THE ENGLISH CATHEDRALS

THE BRITISH ART AND BUILDING SERIES

BRITISH ARCHITECTS AND CRAFTSMEN

By SACHEVERELL SITWELL

Medium 8vo   *Fourth Edition*

THE REGENCY STYLE

By DONALD PILCHER

Medium 8vo

THE OLD CHURCHES OF LONDON

By GERALD COBB and SIR GEOFFREY WEBB

Medium 8vo   *Third Edition*

STUART AND GEORGIAN CHURCHES

By MARCUS WHIFFEN

Medium 8vo

ENGLISH CHURCH MONUMENTS, 1510–1840

By KATHARINE A. ESDAILE

Medium 8vo

GOTHIC ENGLAND

By JOHN HARVEY

Medium 8vo   *Second Edition*

IN PREPARATION

BRITISH NINETEENTH CENTURY
ARCHITECTURE

By REGINALD TURNOR

THE AGE OF WREN

By RALPH DUTTON

THE TUDOR RENAISSANCE

By J. LEES-MILNE

BATSFORD BOOKS

1 SALISBURY CATHEDRAL FROM THE CLOISTERS

*From a watercolour
by J. M. W. Turner
(1796-97)*

THE ENGLISH CATHEDRALS

Photographed by

Herbert Felton

and with a text by

John Harvey

B. T. BATSFORD LTD

LONDON   NEW YORK

TORONTO   SYDNEY

Other Works by John Harvey
    HENRY YEVELE
    GOTHIC ENGLAND
    THE PLANTAGENETS
    DUBLIN
    THE GOTHIC WORLD (*in preparation*)

First Published, 1950

MADE AND PRINTED IN GREAT BRITAIN. TEXT
BY THE ABERDEEN UNIVERSITY PRESS LTD.
ABERDEEN, PLATES BY THE RICHMOND HILL
PRINTING WORKS LTD., BOURNEMOUTH
FOR THE PUBLISHERS, B. T. BATSFORD LTD.
LONDON: 15 NORTH AUDLEY STREET, W.1
AND MALVERN WELLS, WORCESTERSHIRE
NEW YORK: 122 EAST 55TH STREET
TORONTO: 103 ST. CLAIR AVENUE WEST
SYDNEY: 156 CASTLEREAGH STREET

WRITER'S PREFACE

BOOKS about the English cathedrals are legion, and range from the richly illustrated folios and quartos of the nineteenth century down to guide pamphlets. It would seem that little more could remain to be done, save for the dotting of 'i's' and crossing of 't's' in matters of history and dating. Yet it is a singular fact that very few indeed of the existing works have dealt with our cathedrals as a unity ; almost all have been content to accept them as units, and to give their several histories and descriptions with only a certain amount of cross reference from one to another. They have, too, been approached from many angles, the historical and the strictly architectural predominating, with some consideration of their liturgical use. It has not been common to regard them primarily as a series of related works of art : art consecrated to the service of God, truly, but still best to be apprehended as the creation of inspired human genius.

It is, after all, in this way that we appreciate the Masses of Byrd and Palestrina, the Passion Music of Bach, or the symphonies of Haydn. And to the Middle Ages, that ill-defined period which for England means the five centuries from Edward the Confessor to Henry VIII, the cathedral was the ruling art-form, as the symphony was in the Age of Taste. But there is this difference, that the symphony remains purely an art-form, while the cathedral is at the same time the outward and visible sign of an inward life ; a shell made with hands, but still as natural a growth from the spiritual, invisible existence within as the chrysalid is from the butterfly in metamorphosis. However much room for admiration there may be in our post-mediaeval buildings, regarded purely as architecture, it remains true that they never, or hardly ever, can by the wildest stretch of imagination be said to stem from the soul and spirit of the people. I do not here use the word " people " in its modern jargon sense, implying the masses as opposed to the classes, but as meaning the totality of the English community, bred in England and sharing the new, fresh English tradition which in the Middle Ages had only just emerged as a reality, and had not had time to grow stale.

It was during those Middle Ages that the modern nations took their rise, and from her island position, the close kinship of her folk, and the strength of her kings, England was the first of them all. We may therefore expect, and do find, that in English mediaeval art there is a greater unity, less diversity, of style than in any other country ; yet, paradoxically, no country is so rich in variety of artistic invention. Steeped in one tradition, not torn between several, as were the French, the Germans, the Italians, the Iberians, and the Scandinavians, the English were able, within their all-rounding unity, to devote their time and energy to particular developments of tower and front and porch and vault and tracery ; roof, pinnacle, niche and statue ; painting, glazing and decoration of every kind.

Of this diversity of invention and unity of purpose the English cathedrals are the highest examples : the most complete and fully developed summation. The cathedral of the Middle Ages reigned supreme as the chief of all art-forms, the co-ordinating centre of all spiritual culture. Greater than other churches in quality as well as in size, the cathedral was not a church alone : it was the greatest of art galleries, the noblest of lecture halls, sublimest of opera houses. The best of sculpture, of painting, of music and of verse were not too good for its service. Its enrichment provoked the finest flights of the decorative artists. It was in the cathedral, above all buildings, that architecture was truly the mistress art. And from this it follows that in the study of European and of English art and culture, chief place is taken by the cathedral.

Every serious student will wish to visit the cathedrals for himself ; but much can be seen in photographs that is not normally visible on the spot. Much too can be learnt from the study of photographs correlated with written history, both before and after visiting the buildings. And in studying the whole body of English cathedrals as a unity, it is clearly desirable that the photographs themselves should form one whole and represent the viewpoint of a single artist. In the present series of views and details by Mr. Herbert Felton this end has been attained for the first time.

To the many persons who have indirectly contributed to this book I can give only a general acknowledgment ; but I wish to thank especially the vergers and architectural and building staffs of various cathedrals for much kindness and help. To Mrs. M. E. Clegg and to Mr. D. F. Findlay I owe a special debt for the generosity with which they placed unpublished material from the Exeter fabric rolls at my disposal. My wife has throughout given her constructive criticism and advice, and has read the proofs. To my publishers I am grateful not only for valuable assistance, but in particular for their generous permission to reproduce seven of the plans from their book on *The Cathedrals of England*.

J. H. H.

HALF MOON COTTAGE,
BOOKHAM, SURREY.

PHOTOGRAPHER'S FOREWORD

By Herbert Felton, F.R.P.S.

THIS book was envisaged as a folio of plates depicting the beauty to be found in our cathedrals, but fate (in the shape of Mr. Harry Batsford) decreed otherwise, and the excellent text of Mr. John Harvey in conjunction with the photographs presents a new and most fascinating thesis on the development of our major cathedrals.

For many years it had been a great privilege after tea with my dear old friend the late Frederick H. Evans (an Honorary Fellow of the Royal Photographic Society) to browse over and discuss with him the folios of platinum prints of cathedrals and chateaux he made in the late nineties and the opening years of this century.

His prints one would describe as being not so much photographs of actual places, but rather as pictures imbued with the spirit and atmosphere peculiar to each building.

Being a very keen photographer and inspired by the poetry of Evans's work, in 1938 and 1939 I devoted much time and study to the photographic reproduction of effects of light and shade in our various cathedrals —it was the lighting effects I sought, and not a detail photographic survey of the building.

I very quickly discovered that the major difficulty lay in reproducing the extremely long tonal scale inherent in this class of work, ranging from white sky as seen through a clear glass window, to that dull velvet-like quality to be found in the shadows, full of faint detail which could not be represented on paper as a black blotch, but which had to contain at least some very faint indication of what the eye could barely discern.

The ordinary panchromatic plates I was using were useless, so I persuaded the plate manufacturers to provide me a special coating much thicker and richer in silver than those I had been using ; these new plates gave such excellent results that it was simple to make contact prints from the whole-plate negatives on normal bromide.

Since those days new developing reagents have become available, and I have evolved a developer which gives me such perfect negatives with pans (Schiner 25) that eighty per cent. can be enlarged from $\frac{1}{4}$ plate to practically any size with a 500 watt condenser enlarger on normal bromide. All plates are of course backed, and receive individual attention in development.

Most of the general interiors are from whole-plate negatives, but details and interiors of Bath, Bristol, Southwark and Lichfield are from whole-plate prints enlarged from $\frac{1}{4}$ plate negatives.

A word of warning to amateur photographers inspired by the plates to emulate and improve upon this type of work. A rising front is absolutely essential ; without it one's work is limited to that which the camera can give you, so in that case, unless you are satisfied with photographing details at eye level, sacrificing vaulted roofs, and only getting in half the east window, my advice, especially if you are a miniature fan, is " leave it alone ".

En passant it is very interesting to note that fifty years have elapsed since Fred Evans startled the photographic world with his prints, and yet no remarkable change has been produced by photographic material, camera or lens manufacturers, in this field of photography, and in spite of the fact that photographers have greatly improved their technique, they are unable to make prints comparable with the platinums of Evans, which definitely had a most intense feeling of sympathetic appreciation of the subject matter before him.

What wonderful buildings they are, each with its own characteristics ! Durham perched on the edge of cliffs high above the River Wear, Salisbury rising out of a lake of emerald green, Lincoln with its three towers rearing its Gorgon head, as it were, out of the mist and smoke of the town, when seen from the high plateau to the north. Ely with its memories of Hereward the Wake, and the flight of Etheldreda to the secluded island in the fens, there to found the Abbey of Ely and be its first Abbess. The east end of Canterbury with its bastion like corona, the aethereal and aesthetic lady chapel of Lichfield, Chichester riding like a ship above the housetops, the gasps of wonder as one enters the west door of Ely at the immense height of the nave, the kaleidoscopic colours from the stained glass windows dappling the walls and columns of Wells, the " Sea of Steps " in the same cathedral leading up to the chain bridge and chapter house, the apparent freshness of Salisbury nave, looking as though it had but yesterday left the builder's hands, the interior of Exeter, which always gives me the impression of being in a petrified forest, Winchester notable for the lovely retrochoir enhanced by those exquisite chantries grouped around the site of the shrine of St. Swithin—one could rhapsodize for ever.

Often I am asked which cathedral I think the most beautiful. This is a question which has no answer—each is equally beautiful. One may have a preference for Norman, Decorated, or Perpendicular and so prefer one to another, but all are equally beautiful.

What happiness and peace envelopes one whilst waiting for some anticipated effect of light ! Time is forgotten, the outer world like a seething maelstrom whirls round the ancient fane, inevitably sucking all those who worship mammon into its bottomless vortex, but inside tranquillity reigns, and as the light slowly wanders from pillar to pillar enriching some carved capital or corbel it lights on, or increasing by contrast rich shadows, or lighting up by reflected light those dark and obscure corners, the mind subconsciously drifts back to the craftsmen who created these lovely shrines out of some nearby quarry which in itself no one would dream of admiring. The pleasure it has given me, and the knowledge of architecture gained in photographing this inheritance of stone, has brought me very close to those old craftsmen, and whenever I smell a guttering candle, I am once again back in the cathedrals, feeling the peace and intimacy of Evensong, sung as the westering sun fills the interior with a warm and mellow glow ; the priest standing at the altar gives his benediction, the service is ended, the candles on the altar are one by one snuffed. The peace of evening descends upon the slowly darkening choir, and as the light fades, choir, chapels retrochoir and ambulatory lose their form, merging imperceptibly into one another. I feel I am indeed an interloper upon hallowed ground, and stealthily steal away, leaving the building to those to whom it belongs to keep their silent eternal vigil.

ACKNOWLEDGMENT

The Publishers wish to express their thanks to the Trustees of the Victoria and Albert Museum for permission to reproduce the painting which appears as the frontispiece ; to Messrs. J. M. Dent & Sons Ltd., for the illustration on page 10 from " York Minister " by Gordon Home ; to " The Builder " for the illustrations on pages 22 and 76 from " The Cathedrals of England and Wales ".

Thanks are also due to the British Railway Executive for permission to reproduce Fig. 126.

The remainder of the photographs were specially taken for the book by Mr. Herbert Felton, F.R.P.S.

CONTENTS

LIST OF PLATES

2   Durham, above the river Wear

3　Durham nave, looking eastward; c. 1099–1128, vaulting later

INTRODUCTION

WHAT is a cathedral? The word is quite often, incorrectly, used of any large church, as of Thaxted in Essex, and Altarnun in Cornwall, "the cathedral of the moors". But we are here restricted to the proper meaning, a church which contains the *cathedra* or throne of a bishop. In fact there was not during the Middle Ages any important difference, apart from the presence of the throne, between a cathedral and a large church belonging to one of certain other types. Architecturally, the churches of the greater monasteries, like Tewkesbury Abbey, or such collegiate churches as Beverley Minster, were of the same type as the cathedrals. That is to say, they were suited to processional and choral services, and the constant round of the *opus Dei*, " God's service "; they were not primarily directed to the needs of a lay congregation. So any structural or artistic consideration of the mediaeval cathedrals necessarily implies comparison with these other churches built with a fundamentally similar purpose.

On the other hand, the present cathedrals of England are not all of this type : modern growth of population has caused the division of ancient sees, and many of the new cathedrals are normal parish churches, in which the bishop's throne and the choir services are functional intrusions. This book, considering the cathedrals as structures and as works of art, has of necessity a restricted scope. On the one hand it deals only with churches which are now cathedrals ; thus excluding Westminster Abbey, a cathedral only from 1540 to 1550 ; but including St. Albans, an abbey church converted to cathedral use in 1878. Conversely, it deals with cathedrals which were built for choir services ; the parochial churches recently erected into cathedrals are thus eliminated. The total number of churches left for inclusion is twenty-seven, and falls conveniently into three groups of nine.

First come those ancient cathedrals which were always, as now, served by bodies of secular clergy, a chapter of canons presided over by a dean : these are Chichester, Exeter, Hereford, Lichfield, Lincoln, London, Salisbury, Wells and York. In the second place come the monastic cathedrals, those which before their " new foundation " by Henry VIII had been served by regular clergy. In these the bishop of the diocese acted simultaneously as abbot of a great religious house, whose internal administration was headed by the prior. At the dissolution of the monasteries, all the monastic cathedrals then existing in England (except Coventry, which shared a diocese with Lichfield, as Bath does with Wells) were transformed into establishments of secular canons, on the same pattern as the first series : Bath, Canterbury, Carlisle, Durham, Ely, Norwich, Rochester, Winchester,

Worcester. All of these had been houses of Benedictine monks, except Carlisle, which belonged to the Augustinian regular canons.

The third group consists of two sections : the five new cathedrals of Henry VIII which (with Westminster) were abbey churches made cathedral at the Dissolution : Bristol, Chester, Gloucester, Oxford, Peterborough. Bristol and Oxford had been Augustinian houses, the rest were Benedictine. The last four of our cathedrals were great churches surviving from the Middle Ages : Ripon and Southwell, always secular foundations ; St. Albans, a Benedictine abbey ; and Southwark, another priory of Augustinian canons. A curious point is that of the twenty-four mitred abbeys whose abbots sat in the House of Lords with the seventeen bishops (Bath and Wells having but one bishop between them) only four became cathedral: Gloucester, Peterborough, St. Albans and, for ten years only, Westminster ; and of only five others is any part of the church still in use.*

Architecturally, the twenty-seven churches comprised in our three groups are the English cathedrals. They form a relatively compact body, having little in common with the parish-church cathedrals such as Coventry, Chelmsford or Wakefield. But they are, as has already been mentioned, very closely related indeed to the non-cathedral greater churches which have by good fortune survived independently from the same period, some in a fragmentary state, and others almost complete. These residual churches could well form the subject of a separate volume, and deserve far more attention than they generally receive. Beverley, Tewkesbury and Westminster Abbey are, it is true, world famous, but there is a long list of former collegiate and monastic churches which are seldom visited in comparison with the cathedrals.†

Altogether, more than one hundred churches must have belonged to the cathedral tradition in English architecture : one quarter are now cathedrals, one quarter are totally destroyed, and the other half are wholly or partially in use, or represented by extensive ruins such as those of Fountains, Kirkstall and Rievaulx abbeys. This number is small compared with the vast total of

* Crowland, Malmesbury, Selby, Shrewsbury, Thorney. The others were Abingdon, Bardney, Battle, Bury, Canterbury St. Augustine's, Colchester, Evesham, Hulme St. Benet's, Glastonbury, Ramsey, Reading, Tavistock, Winchcombe, Winchester Hyde Abbey, York St. Mary's.

† In addition to the three famous churches named above, and the remains of five mitred abbeys mentioned in the previous note, there are the following complete or fragmentary churches in use : Abbey Dore, Arundel, Binham, Blanchland, Blyth, Bolton, Boxgrove, Bridlington, Brinkburn, Bristol St. Mary Redcliffe, Cartmel, Chester St. John's, Christchurch, Dorchester, Dunstable, Hexham, Howden, Lanercost, Leominster, Malton, Great Malvern, Milton, Norwich Blackfriars, Ottery, Pershore, Romsey, St. Bees, St. Cross, St. German's, Sherborne, New Shoreham, Smithfield St. Bartholomew's (London), Waltham, Wimborne, Worksop, Wymondham.

4 Durham choir; 1093–1099, vaulting later

5　Lincoln from the north-west; central tower 1306–11, by Richard of Stow

cathedrals which existed upon the continent. In England there are only two archi-episcopal provinces ; the area of present France (four times the size of England) was comprised within fifteen mediaeval provinces. The English provinces were made up of fourteen and three sees respectively, while in France the larger number would be near the average. In consequence, the English average of quality is relatively very high ; for though we are accustomed to think of the vast cathedrals of the Île-de-France and Champagne as typical of France, many of the ancient French cathedrals are architecturally insignificant, and have little to do with the main development of the cathedral as an art-form.

The great provinces of France were almost separate countries, and their arts and architecture were correspondingly diverse ; in sharp contradistinction to this, English political unity achieved very early in her history, brought with it a fundamental unity of art history, which nevertheless did not lead to a monotonous uniformity. On the contrary, though the English cathedrals form a homogeneous series, and the French do not, there is within this unity a greater diversity of individual treatment than in, for example, the great churches of the northern French Gothic. French logic and mental clarity were carried to such an extreme that the ideal of one perfect solution, and one only, of any problem was always kept in mind. The commonsense Englishman, working by rule-of-thumb, was not deterred by theory from doing just what he liked. The result is that England has no perfect type cathedral to set beside Chartres or Rheims ; she has no portentous and structurally unsound extravagance such as Beauvais ; no exquisite aspiration like Bourges.

The English temperament is uneasy upon the heights ; at its best it still remains human, not bound to the earth, but firmly rooted in it ; even in its flights of idealism it shuns the purely mystical abstraction and seeks some practical expression of its fervour. Like the ideal Chinese mirrored in Confucius, the Englishman rarely speaks of spiritual beings. Hence there is a warmth, a welcoming and homely quality in the English cathedrals which cannot be found elsewhere. French cathedrals dominate by their remoteness ; German cathedrals crush by sheer superhuman size and strength ; Spanish cathedrals are the dark and throbbing heart of a sombre mysticism ; Italian cathedrals the theatrical properties of children at play. But the cathedrals of England took as their theme the exhortation to the weary and heavy-laden : the man of George Herbert's vision was an Englishman ; deprived of rest in the outer world of everyday affairs, he would be driven to seek it in the church, and above all in the cathedral.

It has to be admitted that in modern times the English have ceased to find their home in the cathedrals ; but the form taken by the buildings themselves was due to this temperamental need of the English character. We must study them, first as works of man dedicated to the constant service of God ; and secondly as works of Englishmen made to be transcendental homes. Thus they typify in the highest degree the English sense of balance which has been our greatest asset and the source both of our worldly successes and of what is best in our character too : a feeling akin both to the moderation in all things inculcated by the Greek, and the doctrine of the golden mean taught by the Chinese sage.

Yet English art too has its excesses ; and in order to live, it is evident that all art must in some way depart from a mere state of equilibrium if it is to avoid the insipid balance of mediocrity. In a purely material sense, the individual excesses of the great nations of Europe can be traced in the extreme characteristics of their cathedrals : France excels in height, Germany in volume, Spain in area, Italy in colour. The English tendency is to length, in its churches as in its anglers' captures, or in those legendary " Tales of the Long Bow " so well epitomized by the authors of *1066 and All That* in their version of Robin Hood's last shaft, which " hit the Sheriff of Nottingham again ".

Remembering that length without breadth is the property of the line, it can be seen that English length is essentially the outcome of the linear quality of our art (16, 63, 140). All the great achievements of our architecture, the finest features of our cathedrals, can be traced back to this preoccupation with outline and with the patterns formed by lines. And the principal, the main lines had to be straight lines. Thus we reached the typically and exclusively English development of the Perpendicular style, where straight lines subdivide windows, and equally form a pattern of blind tracery upon the surfaces of walls (40, 132, 135). Even in arches, where the form resisted to the utmost any attempt to reduce it to straight lines, we invented first the acute and later the obtuse four-centred arch, whose curving arcs are minimized. This characteristic is seen in pronounced form in the acute vault of the nave of Winchester Cathedral (144), and in the obtuse vault, a century later, over the Divinity School at Oxford.

Before examining the chief features of the English cathedral, it may be well to consider briefly the outstanding qualities of the cathedrals of other European countries. To compare only buildings that are comparable, we must set aside the classical survivals and early revivals of Italy, and the Byzantine domed types which spread from the Eastern Empire through Venice to southern and western France. The remaining cathedrals are a family, a north-west European group of buildings sharing a common origin in the Lombardic and Romanesque churches of the early Middle Ages, and grounded in a common tradition of development. Most of these churches, even where they have retained some part of the Romanesque fabric of the tenth to twelfth centuries, have been profoundly modified, if not entirely rebuilt, after the adoption of the Gothic style.

Gothic architecture, whatever its ultimate sources, was first brought to something approaching an integrally fresh style upon French soil, though a major part of its invention is closely linked to England and to Normandy and the dominions of the English kings in France. While admitting the claims of France, or rather of the restricted domain of the French king close to Paris, to be the fountain head of the great Gothic movement which in the thirteenth century was to spread the new art all over western Europe, we must not forget that it was in England and to be specific, in the nave of Wells (52, 54) and the choir of Lincoln, both designed before 1200, that Gothic was first seen in a pure form, freed from survivals of Romanesque massing and detail. Among surviving works, the definite break with the Romanesque tradition is seen to have taken place between the design of the classic works of Sens, Laon and Paris cathedrals and the church of St. Remi at Rheims, and that of the choir of Wells. The vital date is close to 1175, or roughly half a century from the first appearance of the germs of Gothic architecture.

The epoch of the great cathedrals of northern France had really opened with Notre-Dame at Paris, begun in 1163 ; it lasted for about one hundred years. These cathedrals share a common plan and a common approach to the problems of design. They are broad in proportion to their length, being frequently provided with double aisles which materially simplified the buttress-system. The sanctuary terminates in a semi-circular or polygonal arcade surrounded by ambulatory and by radiating chapels. The transepts are of slight projection or altogether absent, and the crossing is seldom emphasized by a central tower. But externally emphasis is placed on the entrances by the provision of deep porches, usually in threes, flanked by nichework and sculptures of great importance, and surmounted by towers in pairs, sometimes above the transeptal as well as the western fronts.

In proportion to their plan, these French cathedrals were extremely tall. By contrast, the height of the earlier Gothic cathedrals of England was moderate, but their breadth was also less, for single aisles were normal. Transepts were always of strong projection, the central tower was generally the point of greatest emphasis, and the eastern termination was almost invariably square. This was so even when it replaced a Romanesque ambulatory. Transeptal towers were not employed, and western towers seldom competed in importance with the central feature of tower or spired steeple. Only the west front was emphasized, and generally to a much slighter extent than in France : the triple porch was most uncommon.

Very often the main entrance was not through the western doors, as in France, but through a lateral porch on which the finest craftsmanship was expended (61, 128).

Notwithstanding their great height, the French cathedrals rarely stand out from the landscape as well as the English, and for two reasons : first, the greater sharpness and clarity of outline of the English churches; secondly, the much more solid grouping of the town round a French cathedral, contrasting with the relative isolation of the English close (17, 22, 147) or, by accident of history, the levelled space on which the claustral buildings of a monastic cathedral once stood. As we have seen, half of the ancient English cathedrals were monastic foundations, and stood at the centre of enormous institutions. The remaining, secular cathedrals tended more and more to borrow from the monastic type, building equally distinguished chapter houses (18, 69, 90, 100) and cloisters (89), and even adding groups of houses, with hall and chapel attached on quasi-monastic lines, for their minor canons and vicars choral.

In the Low Countries the cathedrals adhere fairly closely to the French model, but tend to lose somewhat in coherence of composition while they gain in profusion of craftsmanship, and particularly in the development of the tower as an end in itself. In this they resembled English and German design, and their central position enabled them to bring together many of the beauties of the surrounding schools. In Germany itself Romanesque forms lingered, and there was no adherence to one type of plan. Apses at both east and west ends ; tri-apsidal terminations of sanctuary and transepts ; and three parallel polygonal apses are found alongside the polygonal "chevet" of French origin. Sheer mass is conspicuous in the greater German cathedrals, and as in England much thought was given to the effect of towers and spires, and to the decorative effect of ribbed vaults. Particularly national is the German hall-church of three aisles of equal height but different span, already employed in the thirteenth century, and towards the end of the Middle Ages becoming normal throughout Germany.

Austria, Hungary and Poland received direct impetus from France, and also further influences from Germany. Scandinavia too received Gothic art direct from France, and also from England, notably in Norway. Franco-Scandinavian influences reached the head of the Baltic, competing with the effects of German expansion and colonization. The number of mediaeval cathedrals in these parts of Europe is comparatively small, and it is impossible to speak of national types. In Italy the influence of classic Rome was always too strong to permit the full development of Gothic style, and most cathedrals of the period are strangely mongrel in effect. Apart from the general substitution of colour decoration for mouldings, and the almost total absence of the flying buttress, there are no major characteristics which define an Italian plan or school of design.

In Spain the case was different. During the Middle Ages the Mohammedan Moors were in full retreat from the Peninsula, and cathedrals were set up in the reconquered territories. For the most part these followed French models closely, and were designed by French architects, but later there was an influx of masters from England, the Netherlands and Germany. The churches are wide-spreading and frequently, unlike those of France, have a central lantern supported on squinch arches above the crossing. Owing to the brilliance of the light, the window openings are usually small and the interiors dark. One of the most widespread features is the series of lateral chapels making a complete circuit of the outer walls, between the buttresses. This occurs both in cathedrals of the normal Franco-Spanish type, and in the aisleless churches of Catalonia and southern France, of which the outstanding examples are Gerona, with its single span of 73 feet, and Albi in France. Both this aisleless design, and the central lanterns, show a preoccupation with space, and with the appearance of spaciousness, otherwise rare in Gothic art except in its later years.

It has been common to describe the English cathedrals with undiscriminating eulogy, or else to depreciate them by means of carefully chosen contrasts with France. Neither of these methods results in a fair assessment of their value, either as witnesses to the English spirit, or as works of art pure and simple. In the last resort, judgment must be a matter of personal taste and opinion, but at least the evidence on both sides should be presented fairly, and given a patient hearing. And first it must be said that condemnation of the English cathedrals is usually abstract, and from the point of view of abstract theory. As abstractions, the great French cathedrals undoubtedly come nearer to perfection than any English example ; yet this remote perfection tends of itself to remove them from the human scale of values to which works of art must be related.

With the outstanding exception of Bourges, the greatest of the French cathedrals are cold and aloof, fired only by a detached mental fervour akin to the passion of the higher mathematician and the astronomer for their lofty subjects. No concession is made to human frailty, the quality of mercy is absent from their terrible judgments upon the puny beings who pass through their doors. At Chartres the glorious windows, many of them given by the gilds of local craftsmen, infuse a different atmosphere ; but the statues of the porches appal the spirit by their chilly disdain of mundane affairs. The French cathedrals fall under the great condemnation of French thought, despite their grandeur and logic : having all things, they yet lack charity.

The strict adherence of French art to prepared schemes of iconography ;

the refusal of the architects to countenance decorative elements such as stellar vaulting ; the overburden of heavy flying buttresses to which they were constrained by insistence upon height : all bear witness to this hidden spiritual weakness in France. In the attempt to scale the heavens, the French cathedrals have lost contact with the earth ; in seeking to express something above humanity they fall, by their almost Pharisaical excess, below the best aspirations of which mankind is capable. As temples of the great God preached by their stones, their glass and their colourwork, they suffer only from the one defect : they desired to be the first and greatest of all.

Having said so much, not in depreciation of the masterpieces of France, but in extenuation of other claims, it is time to look on the other side of the medal. The French cathedrals have all qualities but the one : they are the highest fruit of reason, their structures almost personify for us logic, unity of purpose, a complete and rounded aesthetic. In none of these can their English counterparts hope to compete. For quite apart from the distinctions of national temperament, there is a great historical difference between the English and the French cathedrals. Whereas most of the great French churches were so fortunate as to be completed in one age and according to one design, this is in England an exception of the utmost rarity. There is not a single English cathedral, except the Renaissance St. Paul's, which was built from start to finish under the actual supervision of its original architect. Nor is there any mediaeval cathedral save the latest, Bath, which was in essentials finished according to the intentions of its designer, and still retains those essentials unchanged (150-2).

Most of our cathedrals resemble that other homely product of England, the patchwork quilt. Those which most nearly approach the ideal, in order of date, are : Durham, essentially Norman (2, 3, 4), but with added Galilee (47), eastern chapels (82), and central tower (109) ; Lincoln, an Early English structure retaining a Norman front (5, 48) and with the addition of a Decorated retrochoir (93) ; Salisbury, more mature Early English, but with the major addition of a late Decorated steeple (10, 17) ; Exeter, mostly Decorated, but keeping its Norman transeptal towers (110) and adding a Perpendicular west frontal (133) ; Bristol, Decorated (122-4) but with Perpendicular tower (121) and modern nave. Finally there is Bath (150-2), a work entirely designed by Robert and William Vertue, but not completed until modern times, and suffering from extensive alterations and restorations. All the rest are veritable museums of the periods of English architecture.

We cannot therefore judge our cathedrals as complete, integral works of art : their individual parts have to be assessed on their intrinsic merits, and upon the contribution they make, partly intentional, partly fortuitous, to each building viewed as a whole. To some extent we must even form imaginative dream-pictures of a cathedral completed in accordance with the scheme of certain parts. At Canterbury we may mentally supply a nave in keeping with the French design of the eastern arm, or equally suppose a vast accession of funds to have destroyed this in favour of a total reconstruction upon the lines of the present nave, and to the designs of Henry Yevele. The unfinished crossing arches at Ripon (162) suggest the completion of the late Perpendicular church under the supervision of Christopher Scune. And in almost every case, satisfied with our vain imaginings, we should awaken glad that the buildings are as they are. There is a beauty pleasing to the English temperament even in the variety and the disjointedness. We have no desire to be ruthlessly logical, to decide upon the appropriate scheme and eliminate the rest. We much prefer (and surely our cathedrals are the supreme example of an English habit) to muddle through.

It is unfortunately true that in the nineteenth century there arose a school of architects in England who brought much dire destruction to the cathedrals in the name of uniformity and of restoration to the supposed original concepts of the Gothic designer. It is to be feared that this campaign of holy destruction was partly due to latent Puritanism ; partly also it stemmed from the mistaken desire (very natural in Victorian England) to render the English monuments perfect, and so to surpass the rest of the world. But it did spring too from a real love of our architectural heritage. In condemning the excesses of Sir George Gilbert Scott we should remember that we owe to him and to his capacity for enduring exertion, discomfort and dirt in a good cause, the rescue of the Chapter House of Westminster Abbey. Much painful work by Street is condoned by the loving care he expended on the new nave of Bristol, to make it a worthy prelude to the truncated remains of the original church.

Readers of this book, and still more, visitors to the buildings themselves, must accept the cathedrals for what they are. Here our main attempt must be to trace out the general course of development of their history and design, to show how it was that they became the monuments that we know. Unable to consider them as unities, we may still study their separate parts, and see how the great English architects made constant progress in their individual adaptations of the common tradition to the practical and aesthetic needs of their times. Never content with a method of vaulting, a column, a tower, a pattern of tracery, they used all their ingenuity to improve, to make each new specimen better than the last. And probably the most unusual feature of English Gothic is their continuous success. From Saxon times to the reign of Henry VIII there is no single work at any English cathedral which could be described as decadent. Sometimes inspiration flagged a little ; the steps taken were uneven. But nowhere is there marked retrogression, not a work but bears plainly upon it the mark of a creative imagination.

This was true again of our single cathedral of the Renaissance, Wren's St. Paul's in London (8, 9, 167-70). Bitterly as we may regret the loss of Old St. Paul's, historically and stylistically the most interesting of all our cathedrals, its successor is unmistakably a great building. Even the heartiest loathing for the trappings of the classical revival cannot blind us to the fact that St. Paul's is a masterpiece absolutely in the foremost rank of the world's buildings. And Wren, its designer, never showed to better effect the vigour of his mind and his superb control of materials ; while force of circumstances and the feelings of his clients saw that it was no foreign changeling, but an English cathedral church, that was to stand at the top of Ludgate Hill. Mentally shorn of its surface decorations, St. Paul's is indeed the star witness to the force and value of the English tradition.

York : Saxon sculpture of the Virgin and Child, now in the crypt.

[*Drawn by Gordon Home.*

I

The English Cathedral

THE English cathedrals as they now exist are a series of buildings made up of several groups. We have already seen that these groups correspond to two different original types, and to later additions made in the course of time. Sixteen* of our twenty-seven churches have always been cathedrals, but they do not represent the earliest ecclesiastical division of England. The first Christian missionaries to the Anglo-Saxons found the country divided into a number of kingdoms, presently reduced to seven and thus known as the Heptarchy.† Each converted king granted rights to the missionaries, but naturally these grants were limited by his own frontiers. So it comes about that the boundaries of the older English sees represent a former political division of the country. Thus Canterbury and its early offshoot Rochester shared the kingdom of Kent, and Selsey occupied the whole of Sussex ; Dunwich was the see for East Anglia (Norfolk and Suffolk).

These Saxon dioceses underwent much rearrangement, and it was not until after the Norman Conquest that the distribution of cathedrals became roughly what it was to remain for the rest of the Middle Ages. A number of the Saxon cathedrals had been sited in small country villages, such as Elmham in Norfolk and Ramsbury in Wiltshire. At the Council of London in 1075 it was decreed that all such cathedrals should be removed to large towns, and to this decision we owe the existence of cathedrals at Chichester, Lincoln,‡ Norwich, and Old Sarum, later removed to Salisbury. The diocese of Ely was carved out of Lincoln in 1109, and Carlisle, last of all the mediaeval sees, was created in 1133. Both at Ely and at Carlisle the earliest portions of the existing churches go back to dates before their erection to cathedral status.

Before proceeding to detail the development of the English cathedral through the historical styles, it is necessary to consider the general types into which they fall, the methods by which they were built, and the fortuitous juxtaposition of parts built at different periods. To deal first with the ancient secular cathedrals, only at Hereford do extensive remains exist

* Ely did not become a cathedral until 1109, nor Carlisle until 1133.
† The number of kingdoms changed repeatedly, but the seven which gave rise to the name were : Kent, Sussex, Wessex, Essex, East Anglia, Mercia, Northumbria.
‡ This is uncertain ; but the problem of the " Saxon cathedral " at Stow is a vexed one.

of the Romanesque building (6, 33). At Lincoln there is a west front, much cloaked with later work (48), and at Exeter the strange towers which ended the transepts of the Norman church (110). At Chichester a large part of the church is in fact Norman (11, 66), but has been extensively cloaked with work of later periods. Lichfield preserves foundations of its Norman eastern arm beneath the level of the paving. No type emerges from these scattered remains. Lincoln and Chichester both have paired western towers, Hereford had but one, Exeter its transeptal pair. The eastern terminations are doubtful. Lichfield had an apse with ambulatory; Lincoln apparently a central apse, as had Chichester; Old Sarum was square-ended; Hereford had three parallel apses. The two cathedrals which were originally great secular churches, Ripon and Southwell, differed again: Southwell had the unusual feature of a square-ended sanctuary between apsidal aisles, while Ripon, of later date, was square.

Turning to the monastic cathedrals, the Augustinian houses at Bristol and Carlisle, both relatively late, probably had square sanctuaries from the beginning. Of the Benedictine churches, only Rochester began with a square east end, though Ely is thought never to have completed the apsidal termination of which foundations have been traced. Oxford had a stepped termination, with square east end to sanctuary and aisles, which were kept back one bay. The rest were divided between the two common continental plans of the period, namely the triapsal, with three parallel eastern apses; and the periapsidal, with central apse surrounded by a concentric aisle. The triapsal plans were Durham, Peterborough and St. Albans, with Lanfranc's church at Canterbury. This was rebuilt by Conrad as a periapsidal church, and Chester, Gloucester, Norwich, Winchester and Worcester were periapsidal from the start.

The eastern terminations of several early cathedrals can be discovered from their crypts which still exist in spite of the rebuilding of the superstructures. Excellent examples of this are at Gloucester, Winchester and Worcester, while there are also early crypts at Rochester and York. At Canterbury there is a whole series of subterranean chambers and chapels of various dates (49, 50), including the very important lower Lady Chapel and the beautiful Chantry of the Black Prince. Originally designed on the analogy of Constantine's Church at Bethlehem, to house the chief shrine or object of veneration, crypts in England steadily fell out of use. When the whole tendency of the Gothic age was towards more space, light and air, it is hardly surprising that dark and damp undercrofts with low, gloomy vaults should have been disliked. The only Gothic crypts later than the Transition in the English cathedrals were beneath the choir of Old St.

Paul's and that still extant at Hereford, where the vault may have been intended as a bone-house (7). At St. Paul's it was necessary to accommodate the parish congregation of St. Faith.

All the cathedrals had a central tower, and the usual arrangement was to have two western towers as well. At Winchester, and perhaps also at Gloucester and Norwich, where there are now no western towers, they may formerly have existed. Nothing is known of the original west fronts of Bath, Bristol, Carlisle and Oxford ; Ely has one western tower, like the secular Hereford and some non-cathedral churches such as Wimborne and Wymondham; Rochester, Southwark and Worcester had none. St. Albans, like Winchester, had originally western towers, but they were omitted in rebuilding.

The general picture of English Romanesque cathedrals, though like enough to that of the great continental churches of the same period, does show the beginning of several tendencies which were to grow, and thus to differentiate England from the rest of Europe. The universal emphasis on the central tower, in spite of its costliness, the obstruction caused by its great supports, and the risk of collapse, is the most noteworthy feature. But only second to it is the early appearance of the square east end, which in its earliest examples is quite certainly not due to Cistercian influence. This square eastern termination was in the Gothic period to become the chief mark of the English church, cathedral and other, in contradistinction to the apsidal chevet of the French model. Thirdly, and apparently linked to Saxon precedent, we have the instances of a single western tower ; and another English peculiarity, that of placing a pair of western towers outside the aisles instead of in alignment. This plan was adopted at Wells, at Peterborough, in the original front of St. Albans, and was intended at Old St. Paul's. Abroad it occurs at Rouen, and at Trondhjem in Norway, where it was imitated from Wells.

We now leave the remains of the Romanesque cathedrals to dwell at greater length upon their Gothic successors : in most cases, the actual churches we now see. They vary in date from the mid-twelfth century Transitional St. Frideswide's at Oxford (46, 76) to the Tudor Bath Abbey (150-2), begun in 1501, and still unfinished at the end of the age. In all cases but three the extreme east end was square by the close of the Gothic period ; the three exceptions are Canterbury, which has retained its unique circular Corona (63), and Wells and Lichfield, whose Lady Chapels have polygonal terminations (13, 114-16). Norwich now has a somewhat similar modern chapel (41), but this stands on the site of a thirteenth century square-ended Lady Chapel destroyed after the dissolution of the monastery. And Wells, in spite of its polygonal termination, has a square high gable to the retrochoir, behind the Lady Chapel (13). This universality of the English square end contrasts everywhere with continental usage, and goes far to justify the claims of England to a separate Gothic architecture independent of that of France.

The other almost ubiquitous characteristic, that of length, was due in part to the extended naves of the Romanesque churches, adopted by or rebuilt in the Gothic cathedrals. But it was still further emphasized by building eastern extensions equalling or even excelling the total length of the nave. This had already happened at Canterbury by the end of the twelfth century (63) and was to take place everywhere else before the Reformation, except at Salisbury, where the new cathedral was built with the eastern arm slightly exceeding the nave in length ; and Bath, where Bishop Oliver King's church was designed to take up only the length of the nave of the Norman cathedral. Usually the new building at the east

Ely : the "full height throughout" type of design with detached Lady Chapel.

6 Hereford: the Norman south Transept, c. 1100

7 Hereford: the XIII century crypt

8 St. Paul's from the south-east. Designed by Sir Christopher Wren

end entirely destroyed the earlier termination, though Gloucester succeeded in retaining the outer wall of the ambulatory (126), Peterborough the inner arcade with the main apse (15), and Norwich (14, 41) both, merely hewing away the Norman eastern chapel to build a larger rectangular Lady Chapel in its place.

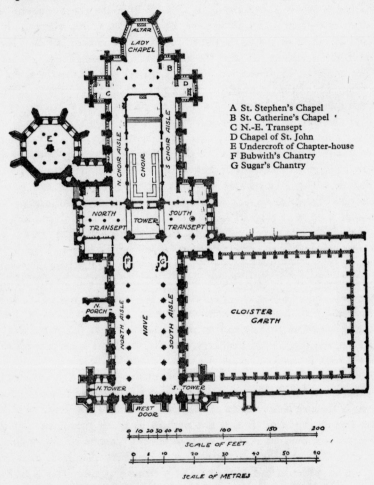

A St. Stephen's Chapel
B St. Catherine's Chapel
C N.-E. Transept
D Chapel of St. John
E Undercroft of Chapter-house
F Bubwith's Chantry
G Sugar's Chantry

Wells : the " lower east end " type of design with polygonal Lady Chapel, octagonal chapter-house and western towers beyond the aisles.

Setting aside the exceptional cathedrals whose high roofs terminate in an apse or polygon of some kind, and discounting Bath, which was the fresh composition of another age, the eastern extensions may be divided into two groups. Furthermore, these groups have a clearly marked geographical distribution. In the one type, the main roof is carried through at its full height to the end, and the east gable rises sheer from the ground to the apex (16). This type is confined to the area north and east of a line drawn from Bowness on the Solway Firth to the Thames at Westminster. South and west of this line the high gable is set back from the east end, which is formed by a Lady Chapel on a lower level (13, 17), leaving space for a raised east window above the high altar. Within the south-western area are three exceptional cases, Worcester, Bristol and Oxford, where the high roof is carried on to the end ; but in each case the eastern bay is aisleless, while in the north-eastern type the aisles continue throughout.

The adoption of the square plan in England was so thorough that it can clearly have been no accident. It is a piece of deliberate policy. That it was not due to any inherent distaste for polygonal forms is proved by the English chapter-houses, which differ from those of the continent in a precisely converse direction. Francis Bond showed convincingly that the reason for the ultimate adoption of the square chevet in England was due to a much stronger emphasis upon correct orientation here than in the rest of Europe. The Romanesque churches with parallel apses had correct orientation of their altars, but were awkward for processions. The periapsidal plan, both in its original Romanesque form, and as developed into the continental chevet, gave completely false orientations. The reason for this great attachment to correct orientation in England may well be due to the force of our pagan traditions. France, and the greater part of western Europe, had been strongly Romanized, and from the fourth century had been continuously Christian. England, on the contrary, was pagan from the fifth to the ninth century, wholly or in part. Great care had to be taken by the missionaries to England to adapt themselves as far as possible to traditional usage, and it seems likely that this would be especially the case with the central feature of solar worship.

But if this is the reason for our strict orientation, it must also account for the other prominent achievement of the square east end : the brilliant lighting of the high altar from an east window, instead of the gloom achieved in the French churches. It was not perhaps so much the desire that the congregation should be able to observe the movements of the celebrant that determined the English method, as the anxiety that both altar and celebrant might be bathed in the rays of the morning sun. This is further borne out by the English provision of eastern or choir transepts, so aligned as to throw still more light upon the altar, as well as to provide the additional subsidiary altars for which they were primarily built. Here again, though choir transepts do occur in France, they were never popular ; their development in England was so marked as to be yet another national peculiarity.

Outside the church itself was the chapter-house, a necessity both for

9 St. Paul's : the dome and nave. Designed by Sir Christopher Wren

10 Salisbury seen across the Avon meadows

11   Western bays of the Norman nave; 1123–48,
     recased 1187–99

12   Across the Transitional retrochoir; 1187–99,
     by Walter of Coventry

CHICHESTER

13   Wells from the east, showing the polygonal Lady chapel
and chapter-house; c. 1293–1319

14 Norwich: the apsidal eastern termination; 1096–1120,
clerestory c. 1362–69

15 Peterborough: the Norman main apse c. 1120; and
Perpendicular retrochoir c. 1496-1508, by John Wastell

16 Ely: the "full height" design of the North and East; retrochoir 1239-50

17 Salisbury : the "lower east end" design of the South and
West, 1220–37. The tower and spire designed by
Richard Farleigh, c. 1334

18 Lichfield: the polygonal chapter-house, c. 1239–49.
Probably designed by Master Thomas the elder

19   The lavatorium

20   The north range; 1421–30, by James Wodrove

21   The east door to the cathedral; c. 1315, by John Ramsey

NORWICH CLOISTERS

22   Lichfield from the north-west.   The west front probably
designed by Thomas Wallace (the Welshman), c. 1280

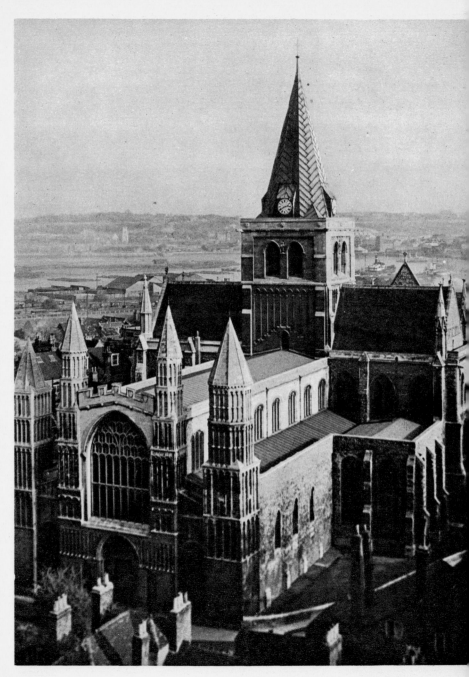

23　Rochester : the Norman west front, c. 1150

24 Rochester: the Norman nave looking east, c. 1115–30

26 Peterborough : the north transept, c. 1117–55

25 Winchester : the Norman north transept ;
1079–93

27 The nave with Bishop Cosin's Carolean font-cover, 1665

28 The apsidal Norman chapter-house, 1133–40

DURHAM

29   St. Albans : the crossing ; 1077–1115, by Master Robert

30 Norwich nave, looking east; c. 1121–45

31   Ely nave, looking east ; c. 1090–1130

32 Carlisle nave; c. 1092–1123

33   Hereford nave, looking east ; 1100–45, altered in the XIX century

34 Southwell nave : the south arcade, c. 1108–50

35 Gloucester nave, looking east; c. 1100–60, vault added 1242–45

monastic and collegiate establishments. In England they were often made the occasion for great artistic display, and the most famous of them are polygonal (18, 69, 90, 100), with vaults either supported on a central pillar, or free-standing. There were not less than 25 of these polygonal chapter-houses in England, and two in Scotland; but more than half have been destroyed. Ten of them are or were at cathedrals within our definition, as well as one at Manchester, of small size. The earliest known is that at Worcester, circular and of ten bays, 56 feet in diameter, and built early in the twelfth century. Next came one now destroyed at Alnwick, Northumberland; those at Margam and Abbey Dore were presumably inspired by Worcester. Then the form suddenly sprang into prominence with that at Lincoln, the largest ever built (59 feet span) (69). So strange a leap in distribution would be hard to understand, if it were not that at that very time the master masons of Worcester and Lincoln Cathedrals both bore the rather unusual name of Alexander. With other evidence suggesting a connection between the two cathedrals at this period, it seems highly probable that the two masters were one and the same man. There is a noble apsidal chapter-house at Durham, and rectangular ones at the monastic cathedrals of Bristol, Canterbury, Chester, Gloucester and Oxford, as well as at the secular Exeter.

The cloisters, universal at monastic cathedrals, and commonly built for show by the secular chapters, are a study in themselves. The development of their design was constant, and shows particularly clearly the extent to which modifications of tradition in one part of the country were watched and adopted elsewhere. Cloisters, or some part of them, remain at Bristol, Canterbury, Chester, Chichester, Durham, Hereford, Gloucester (127), Lincoln, Norwich (19-21), Oxford, Salisbury (89), Wells and Worcester (138), as well as some fragments elsewhere, notably at St. Paul's, London. The secular cathedrals at Lichfield and York never possessed cloisters, while those at Chichester, Hereford and Wells did not form complete rectangles. At Salisbury alone the cloister equalled or surpassed anything produced by the monasteries.

Besides the disappearance of monastic and claustral buildings since the Reformation, there has been another serious loss in appearance suffered by many cathedrals: the destruction of spires. As we have seen, the typical English cathedral had three towers, one over the crossing, and two flanking the west front. Of them all, only one now retains the three spires for which the towers were intended: Lichfield (22). Four central towers have kept their stone spires: Oxford (85), Salisbury (17), Chichester (66) and Norwich (41); there are stone spirelets on the smaller western towers of Peterborough; Durham was preparing to build a stone spire in the early sixteenth century, but never finished it. It is well known that the spire of Old St. Paul's was of timber and lead, and that it was never rebuilt after its destruction by lightning in 1561. According to Stow it was 520 feet high ; and the central spire of Lincoln, blown down in 1584, is said to have been four feet higher still. Lincoln's western timber spires lasted until 1807. Ripon's central spire fell in 1660, and the two on the west towers were taken down four years later. Spires had been removed from the western towers at Durham c. 1657 ; that on the single western tower at Ely lasted until 1801 ; the central tower of Hereford had a timber and lead spire until 1794 (p. 31). Rochester lost its spire in 1830, but regained it in 1904 (23) ; Canterbury's Norman north-west tower was provided with a wooden spire in 1317, which lasted until 1704. The greater north-west tower of Peterborough also had a lead-covered spire ; so had the central tower at Worcester.

In addition to these spires on the churches, there were others upon the many detached belfries which formerly existed, comparable to that which now stands spireless at Chichester. The city parish and friary churches also were usually provided with spires, and the impression of a medieval civic skyline must have been very different from that to which we are accustomed ; only in north Germany and the Baltic was the multitude of spires carefully preserved until modern times. Up to 1942, Lübeck still presented the picture which it made in 1432, when it was painted in the background of an altar-piece now or formerly at Reval, and which showed nine tall spires as well as innumerable smaller ones. The loss of atmosphere and purpose due to this great destruction of spires in England is incalculable ; it amounts to the cancelling of a great part, almost the most symbolic part, of the Gothic message. Even in spite of the Renaissance, Wren was consciously or subconsciously aware of this message when he so designed his London churches as to leave the city with more spires than it had had before the Fire. More recent generations have been content that this message too should be lost in the monstrous upward surge of commercial premises.

From the story of loss and ruin, let us turn to the first building. In an age of cathedrals, how did cathedrals get built ? Not only the cathedral churches themselves as we see them now, but in many cases enormous monastic buildings had to be financed and erected. The sheer size of the greater churches, in England as well as on the continent, was enough to daunt any constructor unendowed with faith as well as self-confidence. The late Professor Prior gave a number of valuable figures for the areas of the greater churches, in illustration of the immense scale upon which the Norman builders worked. The fountain-head of the later Romanesque was the abbey church of Cluny in Burgundy, with an area of 54,000 square feet ; the early Gothic narthex brought the total to 66,000. The largest of the Norman cathedrals in England, Winchester, had been planned originally to cover as large a space, and the abbey church at Bury St. Edmunds was only just under 70,000 square feet. These areas are as large as those of the largest completed French cathedrals ; Cologne was 90,000 ; but even this was surpassed by Old St. Paul's which with its Norman nave and Gothic choir and transepts reached 100,000 square feet. The vast size of Old St. Paul's can be appreciated by comparing it with the 70,000 square feet of Lincoln.

Another of Prior's illuminating comparisons is between the cross-sectional areas of the piers of Durham quire, laid out c. 1093, and those of Canterbury quire of 1175. The Norman pier is seventeen times as big as the early Gothic one ; a disproportion which evidences the enormous advance in constructive skill made in a couple of generations. This advance of skill is also shown by the large number of Romanesque towers which fell down, compared with the astonishing durability of Gothic work. Among the many collapses of Norman towers in England were two at Bury, central towers at Ely, Winchester and Worcester, and the western tower of Hereford (p. 31). There was naturally some trouble in Gothic times, and the first tower at Lincoln fell in 1237, while trouble threatened at various periods at Peterborough, Salisbury, Wells and York. At Chichester the tower and spire actually fell, but after a life of five centuries, comparing very favourably with the fifteen years of the first Winchester tower, and the 200 of Ely.

Both the financing and the practical administration of building on such a scale were great problems. Generally speaking, English administration was more successful than English finance. There is no doubt that much of the patchwork character of our cathedrals is due to the inability of their founders to provide enough cash and credit to complete the work adequately upon the plan adopted. On the other hand it is permissible to wonder whether this was always the explanation. At Gloucester after 1328 the shrine of Edward II is said to have attracted for many years multitudes of pilgrims who made vast offerings to the abbey. Yet the building works actually carried out as a result were surprisingly meagre and slow. Fifty years were taken over the reconstruction, in a skilful but economical manner, of the presbytery (129, 135) and transepts ; in another century only a new cloister (127), a new west front and two bays behind it ; a reconstructed tower (126, 128), and a Lady Chapel of very moderate size had been added (130). The offerings at Becket's shrine were astronomic, but never resulted in total rebuilding of Canterbury.

A suspicion is felt that the mediaeval clients and their building masters were less iconoclastic over ancient work than is often alleged. There were certainly prelates and others who wished to be in the front of fashion ; but others loved the old churches they knew. It seems almost certain that the preservation of vast Norman churches at Durham, Ely, Norwich and Peterborough, and the early Gothic work at Canterbury, was due as much to affection as to lack of means. The careful adherence to earlier plans at Westminster Abbey and Beverley Minster, and the provision of a new porch scrupulously framing the precious Norman doorway of Malmesbury Abbey, point in the same direction.

Besides the offerings of pilgrims, funds were provided by wealthy lay-men, anxious to take out a spiritual insurance policy ; by bishops and abbots fond of their church, or of ostentatious temperament ; by rents of endowed property ; by casual gifts and bequests ; and by carefully planned public appeals. These last were a most important method of attracting money, then as now, but contributions secured a definite return in masses and prayers, and other spiritual privileges for the donors. The chapters, secular and monastic alike, placed a responsible official in charge of these funds, and subjected his accounts to annual audit. There were two main methods of organizing the actual work of building ; by direct labour, and by contract. In the direct labour system (which was the earlier), the administrator, possibly one of the monks or canons, had himself to arrange the purchase and transport of materials and the hiring of men. In practice he was able to delegate a good deal of this routine to the technical master of the works, normally an experienced master mason. This master was also the architect to whose plan and details the church would be built. In some cases the chapter appointed one of their number or a clerical official, and the master mason jointly, to have full charge of the work, as happened in the late thirteenth century at Exeter Cathedral.

In practice, the direct labour system was frequently modified by the introduction of task-work, when individual craftsmen were paid lump sums for performing set tasks, such as the cutting of so many feet of a moulded string-course, or erecting so many perches of plain walling. Gradually the tasks became larger, and were introduced by written undertakings on the part of the craftsman to do the work to time, and of the client to pay the agreed sum at stated dates. By these stages the older methods gave place to the contract system more or less as we know it today. At the English cathedrals little major work was done by contract, though by the late four-teenth century prominent masons undertook large tasks : at Old St. Paul's in 1388 Henry Yevele was paid the last instalment for his new front of the south transept. The whole task amounted to nearly £300, or in our values about £20,000 to £25,000.

In the early Middle Ages it was customary for the master to reside at the job, and have full and constant control ; later on, and certainly before the end of the thirteenth century, he had become a supervising visitor. This implied that he had control of more than one job at once, and the necessary corollary was a permanently resident undermaster or warden of the works on each job. For the work at Old St. Paul's above mentioned, Yevele's friend and junior partner, and later his successor as King's Master Mason, was his warden : Stephen Lote. Both master and warden were bound by craft custom to take up an absolutely impartial position as between the interests of the client and those of their fellow-craftsmen, an interesting precursor of modern architects' etiquette, between client and builder. The warden had charge of the working masons who cut their stones beneath the shelter of a hut or open-sided pentice known as a " lodge ". At the great cathedrals the lodges became permanent institutions, though the staff employed might fluctuate from one or two up to 100 or more, according to the available money and the time of year.

Besides the masons, a master carpenter had charge of a staff of carpenters to provide scaffolding, centrings, the wooden roofs, and later the choir fittings and doors. Glaziers might be directly employed, or the work might be sent out to glass-painters who had their own shops in the city. But in any case close touch had to be kept, that the glaziers might be provided at the right time with cartoons showing the exact size of the window openings they were to fill. The making of plans, details and cartoons went on in a separate room or shed known as the " trasour " or tracing-house. Here there were drawing boards on trestles, and in some cases at least, a large slab of plaster-of-Paris, on which full-size details could be set out with the help of a great pair of 3-foot dividers. Elsewhere, stone paving slabs have been found with the geometrical setting-out lines scratched upon them. At least one smith would be kept busy on the constant re-sharpening of the masons' tools, and the provision of necessary ironwork. Besides nails, hinges and stay-bars for the windows, this often included heavy wrought-iron bars of considerable length, for use as exposed tie-bars or as hidden reinforcement.

The master mason would have to visit quarries to find suitable sources of stone, and the carpenter would mark timber in the forests to be felled by his men. The clerical chief arranged transport for these and other materials, and to keep the works running smoothly, had to give gratuities at suitable moments, and at such occasions as the turning of a great arch, the setting of a keystone, or the laying of lead on the roof, distribute a generous portion of ale, or even a full meal, to all hands. Work tending to be intermittent, it was not always easy at short notice to raise the necessary number of men, and in some instances the church authorities were able to obtain a writ of impressment from the king, by which their officer was enabled to conscript workmen of the right types, up to a maximum number. These conscripts had to be paid at the normal rates, and also allowed " prest-money " according to the distance they had to come, just as if they had been taken into the king's own service.

Rates of progress differed enormously : the whole eastern arm of Canterbury (63-5), was rebuilt in the ten years 1175-1184 ; the Lady Chapel at Salisbury (75) took five years, and the rest of the church another forty altogether. On the other hand, the small cathedral of Exeter was about a century in its rebuilding, and the nave of Westminster Abbey was still not completed after 270 years of intermittent work. The great speed of the faster works, and their immense capacity of endurance, prove that neither jerry-building nor incompetence can have been common. The cathedrals of the Middle Ages are among the soundest, as well as the greatest of the works of man.

St. Albans : the Ramryge Chantry.

[*Drawn by Roland W. Paul.*

II

NORMAN CATHEDRALS

ALTHOUGH cathedrals of the Saxon period existed on the sites of many of our present cathedrals, they have left hardly any remains apart from foundations not actually visible. The one outstanding exception is Ripon, where the existing crypt is said to have been built about A.D. 670 for St. Wilfrid. Its central chamber and wandering passages are strangely reminiscent of the grottoes beneath the Church of the Nativity at Bethlehem; the same arrangements are found at Wilfrid's other surviving crypt beneath Hexham Abbey. It is a strange coincidence that the shipwrecked Gaulish bishop, Arculf, should at this very time have been relating his travels in the Holy Land, and setting down plans of the sanctuaries in Iona, whence the narrative was sent to York as a gift to the Northumbrian King Aldfrith.

It is also disputed whether there may not be certain late Saxon work in the crypt at Gloucester, but on the whole it is safe to consider as our earliest cathedrals those built after the Norman Conquest of 1066. The first of the great churches built in the Norman form of Romanesque was the new abbey at Westminster founded by Edward the Confessor in 1050 and consecrated in 1065. Of the existing cathedrals, those with a mainly Norman structure are St. Albans (29, 37-8), Rochester (23-4), Durham (2-4, 28, 47), Norwich (14, 30, 41) and Peterborough (15, 36, 154), with extensive parts of Chichester (11, 67) and Worcester. Ely and Gloucester are also very largely Norman, and Winchester retains its interesting early transepts (25) and crypt. The nave of Old St. Paul's, now totally lost, was one of the most important of all. In spite of variations in detail, there is an astonishingly close family resemblance between all these churches.

In the first place, the Romanesque builders were still extremely ignorant of structural problems and the strength of materials. From this resulted the extreme solidity of the work, which gives to it its leading characteristic : massiveness. The proportion of wall and pier is enormous ; of arch and window relatively slight. This exaggerated the tendencies of Roman and Early Christian basilicas, and produced an effect almost always lacking in grace. Commonly this failing was redeemed by excellent general proportions, and by the cumulative, soothing effect of tier upon tier of round-arched openings. There is another aspect of these buildings which had a practical as well as a spiritual effect. They were not merely churches, but in an age of insecurity, strongholds against savagery and barbarism. The thick walls could not easily be undermined ; the small openings were easily defended. Here was at least a spiritual line of descent from the catacombs.

Being a direct importation from Normandy, our Romanesque cathedrals have little about them that is exclusively English. They are not, at any rate not to a significant extent, national works of art. They belong to European history, and especially to the history of Benedictine monasticism. For even the secular cathedrals of the late eleventh and twelfth centuries reflected in great measure the traditions of the monks' churches. It was an age dominated by the Benedictine Order, and its Cluniac offshoot. Through five centuries of storm and stress, human values in western Europe had been preserved within the thick walls of the monasteries, and they were now being given out again to the public through the medium of the great churches. The age of monastic domination was passing away, but it was still able to build its enormous temples from end to end of the new country conquered for continental civilization.

It is significant that all the great churches which remain largely Norman in structure were monastic ; while among our Gothic cathedrals it is the collegiate foundations that predominate. The concentration of influence and money in the hands of the Benedictines typified the earlier period ; by the later twelfth century, when the new Gothic was sweeping the western world, it was the courtier-bishops who were in power. While the architecture of the thirteenth century was to express the relation of free men in a free world, bound together by the love of God, the Norman cathedrals show us the huddling together of wretches crazed by fear of the outside world, its murder and rapine. It is too easily forgotten that England had nearly fallen a prey to yet another assault of Scandinavian Northmen immediately before Hastings. That England was to be a part of civilization, not of splendid savagery, was due as much to the usurper Harold's success at Stamford Bridge, as to his failure at Senlac. The Normans were already Northmen at several removes.

The dark world of outer barbarism was, nevertheless, still present in men's minds. Not until the fresh knowledge and the new Gothic spirit swept Europe in the succeeding century, were men to feel that they lived in a bright and open world. The sombre gloom of cave-dwelling and cave-worship hangs over the monks' choir of St. Albans (29), the long nave of Peterborough (36) ; flickers like a grey shadow glimpsed from the corner of an eye in the transepts of Winchester (25). Dark enough now, but with the opacity of early glass midnight must have reigned at noon. Most early windows, too, have been enlarged. Where, for climatic reasons, no floods of sunlight were allowed to enter even a Gothic church, we may recapture the intensity of this artificial night : as within Barcelona Cathedral. Better still, at the Church of the Holy Sepulchre, owing to the blocking of windows, the ambulatory is in total darkness, save for the sparks of wicks in oil, and the guttering candles of pilgrims and processions.

The outstanding achievement of northern art in the Middle Ages, and nowhere more than in England, was the progressive freeing of churches from this atmosphere of the cell. The surest index of the movement of the times is the amount of new light admitted as one generation succeeded another. The ability thus to admit more light depended entirely upon advancing knowledge of construction and materials. The progress of knowledge was at first gradual, and resulted from experience of successes and failures in a large number of buildings all over northern Europe, but particularly in north France and in England. There can be no doubt that even in the Romanesque period there was a good deal of international intercourse among craftsmen, and the political link between Normandy and England inevitably caused much coming and going.

Of all the greater structural problems, that of providing a permanent stone covering was the greatest. And so difficult was the task considered in northern Europe that even where vaults of small span were built in crypts and aisles, the high clerestories of the churches were very seldom vaulted. There is no example of a groined high vault in England, and even when the ribbed vault was introduced at the end of the eleventh century at Durham (3, 4), it found few imitators. The only Romanesque high vaults in England, other than those of Durham and its neighbour Lindisfarne, which (so far as the evidence goes) may have existed, were at Hereford and Gloucester choirs. A vault was also put up over the old nave at Lincoln in the 1140's, on the threshold of the Gothic period. Nor was this lack of vaults the result of failure ; it is plain from the plans of piers and shafts that vaults were never intended. In striking contrast, vaults formed an integral part of the scheme at Durham from its inception in 1093. Durham is therefore our only cathedral presenting a complete Romanesque scheme, perfect in all its parts (2, 3, 4, 28, 47).

Like many other Norman churches, the bay-design at Durham is of the double variety : only the alternate piers carry the vault, and are compound. The intermediate supports are great cylindrical columns (3, 4). Even where there was no vault to carry, shafts were often carried up from base to summit of the wall inside the piers, and this gives a typical Norman scheme found at Ely (31), Old St. Paul's, Norwich (30), Peterborough (36) and Winchester, as well as at St. Albans, where there are flat pilasters instead of shafts (37). A modified form of this type appears at Rochester, much altered by the work of later periods (24) ; before the even greater changes at Chichester (67) its arcades were probably similar.

The other great type of Norman arcade is found at Carlisle (32), Hereford (33) and Southwell (34), and consists of rather short cylindrical columns supporting a narrow strip of plain wall, on which stands a second range of triforium arches, and above these a range of clerestory

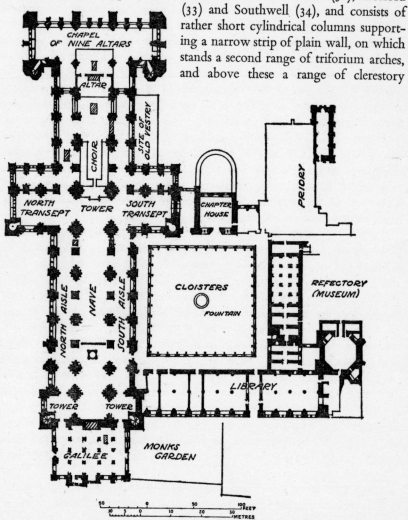

Durham : the most complete Romanesque cathedral, with western Lady Chapel and later cross-eastern termination.

openings. In this scheme there is no accentuation of the vertical bays, but a strong horizontal emphasis on the level line at the top of each stage. The same scheme was followed at Gloucester, but with a very big difference :

the columns were made extremely tall in proportion to the height of the small triforium and moderate clerestory (35). This design, also followed at the neighbouring Tewkesbury, lessened the extreme horizontality of the walls and threw a cross-emphasis upon the height of the very tall side-aisles.

Durham apart, none of the Romanesque cathedrals can be considered remarkable as examples of design. Even such an idiosyncrasy as that of Gloucester and Tewkesbury, though it indicates an individual brain at work, does little to remove the church from its class. For this reason the anonymity of the Norman cathedrals is the less to be regretted. Even so, it is not to be supposed that in either the eleventh or the twelfth century such great buildings were put up without the intervention of an architectural supervisor. Amateurish as are some of the early methods when judged by the Gothic standards of 1150-1550, they still required a high degree of competence and organizing skill. Nor, in talking of anonymity, must we be misled into thinking that literally no names have been preserved. In several cases it is possible to connect the name of a master with the church he built.

Before the Conquest, Godwin Gretsyd had been the master mason of the Confessor's new abbey at Westminster, and was apparently a benefactor of Hyde Abbey at Winchester, as both he and his wife were to be prayed for there. Next comes the outstanding personality of Robert, the master of St. Albans Abbey from 1077 until 1100 or so. "He excelled all the masons of his time", we are told by the chronicle of the Abbots, and considering the ingenuity as well as the beauty of his re-use of Roman materials, there is some truth in the statement. His employer, Abbot Paul, gave him for his skill and labour lands to the astonishing value of 60s. (say £300 or more) yearly ; but the monastery murmured against so princely a gift, and Robert on his deathbed honourably restored the land to the abbey, renouncing the claims of his heirs. But he seems to have had another grant of land at Sopwell worth 8s. (£40 or so) a year, from Paul's successor, Abbot Richard. Robert, or Rodbert as he is also called, must in any case have been well off, for in the list of benefactors he is recorded not only to have worked faithfully about the building of the church, but to have contributed 10s. every year as long as he lived. At that date such a sum cannot have been worth less than £50 in our values, and was probably a great deal more.

At the building of Prior Ernulf's new choir at Canterbury, between 1096 and 1107, one Blitherus was the "most accomplished master of the craftsmen" ; and in 1127 a certain Andrew was mason of St. Paul's in London. Very likely he was the architect of the nave, which had been begun about 1110. Scanty as are these notices of the builders of our Norman cathedrals, they are enough to show that even then the masters in charge of the work were men of standing and highly esteemed. They could, and in some cases did, become wealthy, as we know their Gothic successors did. And these few are the first trickle of the flood of hundreds of the mediaeval masters known to us by name.

The interior of the Norman cathedral is best conveyed by Peterborough (36, 154), for not only does it remain unvaulted, but it has retained most of its great apse. Everywhere else the insertion of Gothic windows or the total reconstruction of the eastern arm has made it impossible to visualize the eastward view. The effect is cumulative : bay follows bay as the vast naves drag their slow length along : ten bays at Peterborough, twelve at Ely, fourteen at Norwich. In the "horizontal" design, with three separate and superimposed storeys, the churches are much smaller, and one may wonder whether this design were not actually adopted to increase the perspective effect of length (32-4). In the monks' churches a solid screen wall divided the parochial nave from the convent choir, an effect which can still be seen in Romanesque naves at Norwich (30) and St. Albans (37). This interruption of the vista has caused much controversy, not only in modern times. In the early twelfth century Abbot Suger swept away the interruption of a screen-wall from the ancient church at St. Denis. In our own time it has been done by Sir Ronald Storrs when governor of Jerusalem, at the Bethlehem Church of the Nativity. Since the Middle Ages a large number of screens have been abolished in "aesthetic" improvements. It is a knotty problem for which everyone must find his own solution, and usually has no difficulty in doing so.

The fragmentary state of most of our Norman cathedrals makes it difficult to discuss the intentions of their designers. I have already referred to the standard type of external scheme, having in its perfect form three towers, one central and two western, and all surmounted by spires. In Norman times the spires were generally of rather low pitch, and at Southwell the modern spires on the two western towers are believed to be accurate reproductions of the original ones * (51). Southwell is in fact our only cathedral to preserve all three Romanesque towers, dating from the first half of the twelfth century. Owing to the rather small scale of the church, they hardly compare with what must have been intended at the greater cathedrals, but they do give a faithful picture in outline, as seen from western viewpoints.

Until 1834, long enough for Britton to have made measured drawings of it, an original Norman tower stood at the north-west corner of Canterbury Cathedral, the only survivor of the old nave. As in the case of the Southwell towers, it had clasping buttresses of slight projection, and stage after stage filled with different patterns of arcading. The smaller towers behind the eastern transepts at Canterbury are variations on the same theme.

* They appear in Kip's view, c. 1724.

A more imposing arrangement of towers and recesses, unique of its time, was carried out at Lincoln, and still exists though much cloaked by work of various later periods (48). The free-standing transeptal towers at Exeter are more massive than the western examples, and have a well-graduated diminution of solid masses towards the top. Beside the light effect of the Gothic church, they appear rather blind and wall-sided.

Of central towers of Norman cathedrals we have three, at St. Albans (38), Winchester (39) and Norwich, the last surmounted by a Gothic spire a little too small for it (41). All three towers are immensely successful, each is absolutely distinct from the others. St. Albans, the earliest of the three, is divided into three storeys of unequal height. In the lowest are blind arched recesses cleverly displaced towards the centre, thus increasing the apparent solid mass at the angles. Next comes a narrow band comprising four round arches on each face, and beneath each arch a pair of sub-arches. Above is another tall stage, with one arch on each side of the central pilaster on each face, each of these being subdivided. The height of this tower above the abbey roofs is perfectly proportioned, and makes the distant view of St. Albans impressive and unforgettable. It was not for nothing that the Abbey boasted of Master Robert.

At Winchester, the first Norman tower fell in 1107, and the present one was built immediately afterwards. Here there is no attempt to dominate the church by superior height, as in Robert's work at St. Albans. The Winchester tower has but one external storey, composed of three tall round-arched windows built in recessed orders, and somewhat set in from the angles of the tower (39). Again the proportions are admirable, and though less ambitious, the result is no less successful than at St. Albans. Lastly, at Norwich we have a far more complicated design arrived at in two stages (41). The lowest storey above the roofs belongs to the original church, built between 1096 and 1119. The angles are surrounded by a mass of attached shafts, giving great strength and emphasis to the verticals. Between these angle-turrets each face of this lowest stage is divided into nine tall openings, of which all but three are blind. Those which are pierced are the second from each end and that in the centre. Above this, and built between 1121 and 1145, is a massive cubical stage, continuing upwards the shafted corners. Between them comes first a series of nine blind arches interlaced with a second series, dividing the wall into eighteen panels altogether. Next is a much taller stage, repeating the motive of nine panels, three of them pierced, but to a larger scale, and with ornament in the blind panels. Above this again comes a set of five panels, each containing two super-imposed roundels, the upper set pierced. The total effect is impressive, but rather indistinct in detail.

All these towers were far surpassed, but not until the Transitional period, by the immense western tower at Ely (43). This is now surmounted by a Gothic lantern, which formerly had a spire. Here the designer profited from travelled observation of the great towers we know, and doubtless others which have disappeared, such as those of the abbey at Bury St. Edmunds. The towered gateway at Bury is, in fact, clearly one of the main sources of the Ely design, giving the superimposed ranges of three windows, interspersed with narrower bands of minor arcading or roundels. The more pronounced corner turrets at Ely derive from Norwich. The whole vast front, with its western transepts as well as the lofty tower, was built in less than a quarter century, from 1174 to 1197. Though in process of translation into the idiom of the pointed arch, the western tower at Ely maintains the massive strength of Romanesque building.

This is also the case at Oxford, where the main structure of the cathedral is Transitional in date, from 1160 onwards. Although retaining round arches, the round columns are more slender (46), and the foliated capitals more dainty. Around the arches are narrower, more wiry mouldings. But the striking feature of Oxford is its unusual bay design, a forerunner of the Gothic attempts to merge the triforium into a vertical scheme. But while the later versions were to succeed by bringing the clerestory down to include the triforium, the Oxford architect had the somewhat unhappy notion of setting back his aisle-vault (76) beneath tall arches which included the height of the triforium in the nave arcade. Unsuccessful as the experiment was, it was one of the necessary stages towards Gothic achievement.

The two great architectural features of the interior were the sanctuary and the bay design. We have seen that, with the partial exception of Peterborough (15, 36), no original chevet of a Norman cathedral exists in a form in which we can appreciate it. The variations of bay design have been discussed. Similarly, we have examined the principal external features, namely the towers. But another feature of the outside which was of special importance even where unemphasized by towers, was the front itself. In general, the Norman churches do not seem to have laid great stress upon the western entrance of the church. There was, it is true, at least the one doorway, but this might not be an outstanding feature. Sandwiched between the two simple towers at Southwell, such a doorway is not impressive. On a rather larger scale, Chichester must have been much the same ; so was Chester before Perpendicular alterations. But there was another type of front, without towers, as at Norwich and Rochester (24) and formerly at Hereford (p. 31). The place of towers was taken by pronounced turrets at the outer angles of the aisles, and there was also some decorative treatment of the ends of the arcade walls of the nave. There might be three recessed doorways, as at Norwich ; or the side archways might be blind, as at Rochester.

Hereford : The Norman west front and western tower which fell in 1786. The spire was taken down in 1794.

[Engraved by T. Harris from a drawing by G. Merricke.

To make up for the lack of towers, these façades gave greater prominence to the doorways themselves. We do not know what the original central porch at Norwich was like, but that at Rochester is a splendid work of soon after the middle of the twelfth century (45). The archway is in five recessed orders, the innermost supporting a tympanum carved in high relief. All five arch-rings are deeply carved, and a carved label-mould crowns all. At Ely the Transitional front is an affair of many superimposed ranges of arcading (43), and the entrance is cloaked by the early Gothic Galilee porch (42). But at Durham the austere Norman front has before it a Galilee of another kind : Transitional, and really a Lady Chapel. Intended for the east end of the cathedral, it was destroyed by the supernatural misogyny of the long-dead St. Cuthbert, who would have no women coming to worship near his bones. Consequently it was rebuilt outside the west doors, where any number of females could assemble without causing the Saint annoyance. Built for Bishop Puiset or Pudsey about 1170, it is one of the latest round-arched buildings at the cathedrals (47). But it bears witness at the same time to the coming of the Gothic spirit in its attenuated columns and fine-cut zig-zags. It was probably designed by Puiset's great master mason, Richard of Wolveston, famous as an architect throughout the north country.

There remains only the front of Lincoln to describe. It is of its own kind, and though it suggested the Gothic front of Peterborough, remains unique. It consists of three deep recesses containing doors, now surmounted by Perpendicular windows ; and at each side two smaller arches leading merely to deep niches (48). The central recess is much the highest. Behind the Gothic arcading which now crowns the work, rise the twin western towers, provided with corner turrets of strong projection. The Gothic extensions to north and south, with their system of arcading carried right across above the earlier recesses, seem to have been designed specially with a view to enshrining the ancient work. Clearly this is an instance where the old work was of such outstanding importance and interest that no one would allow its destruction. It is the only part surviving of the church of Remigius, built between 1075 and 1092. The master who designed this strange and impressive façade, whoever he was, was one of the first in England to strike a fully individual note. Not only this ; his is the earliest solution, and one of the most satisfactory, of the problem of linking the outside of the church to what is within. Taken as a whole, English architecture was less successful in this respect than in most others, and there is some compensation in our possession of Lincoln. Dominant on its hill, Lincoln Minster shows us some of the most glorious lessons of Gothic : but to enter in we must pass through these strange portals, accepted as worthy even by the later builder, Chesterton's Architect of Spears.

Knowing what was to come, we cannot regard the Romanesque cathedrals

36 Peterborough nave, looking east ; c. 1155–75

37   St. Albans nave, showing the rood-screen ; 1077–1115,
screen c. 1360, perhaps by Henry Yevele

38 St. Albans : the tower and south transept, 1077–1115.
Designed by Master Robert

39 The west front. Finished by William
Wynford; c. 1360–1400

40 From the east; presbytery re-fashioned by
Thomas Bertie c. 1520–32

WINCHESTER

41   Norwich: the east end from the north; 1096–1120;
the Lady chapel recent

43   The western tower and transept, c. 1174–97

42   The West porch, c. 1198–1215

Fry

45 Rochester : the Norman west door, c. 1150

44 Ely : the Prior's door, c. 1120

46 Oxford choir, looking east, with its later vault; 1158–80, vault c. 1480, perhaps by William Orchard

47 Durham : the Galilee, c. 1170. Probably designed by
Richard of Wolveston

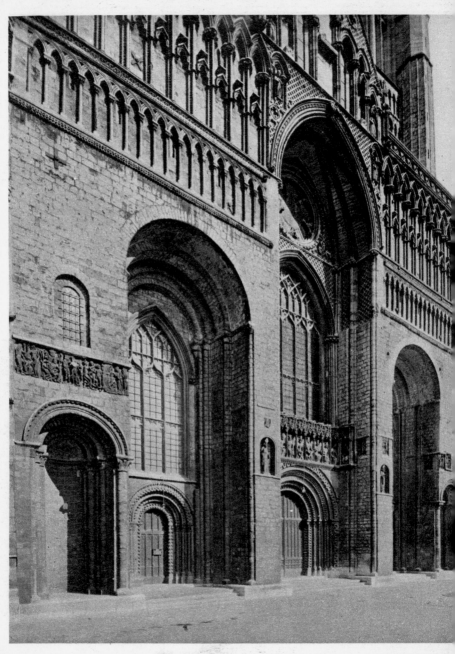

48   Lincoln: the west front, c. 1225–53, with its Norman
core, 1074–92; doorways c. 1140–50

49 The east end of the Chapel of Our Lady of
the Undercroft, screenwork c. 1372–77

50 The crypt of Prior Ernulf under the choir
from the west, 1073–80

CANTERBURY

51   Southwell from the south; 1108–50, the presbytery, c. 1230–50

as an end in themselves. In the curious mingling of styles which is above all typical of the English churches, it is the solemn and massive Norman which provides a foil for the light and airy Gothic. There is something satisfying about the static repose, even heaviness of the solid pillars, the dark aisles, the rough-dressed stones. Perhaps, being Saxon Englishmen and so not very far removed from Normans, we take a kind of pride in their crudity. We like the roughness, the emergent savagery of our Norman buildings. But even viewed from a more reflective standpoint, there is great virtue in the combinations and contrasts of style to which we are accustomed. It is fatally easy for one good custom to corrupt the world, and there is a certain smugness about the highly integrated perfection of some French cathedrals which grates upon us. It is this dehumanized perfection of the highest flights of France (Bourges always excepted) that puts it on a lower level. And we should above all be thankful to our fore-bears for the conservatism with which they held their hands. How easy it would have been to make a clean sweep of Lincoln, for example, and to build a newly designed front at little more cost.

If the preservation of relics of earlier buildings were the result of pure chance in every case, it would indeed be extraordinary how so many vital clues have survived. It is rare for us to lack some evidence, often the most vital evidence, for the forms of the predecessors of our cathedrals. I except the Saxon churches, which admittedly have left little trace. But in most other instances there is enough to piece together the designs according to which successive masters worked. Every one, or almost every one, of our cathedrals is a palimpsest. They have been worked on again and again, by master after master. Each has had in mind his own plan, and probably also that of his predecessor. Some were iconoclasts, others reverent in their handling of old stones, which they preserved and reset as far as possible. Much of the value of our cathedrals, at least to us, is their relative immunity from change.

The outcome of this reluctance to do more than is absolutely needful has given us the cathedrals as we see them. As we go on through the styles, we shall find a queer series of permutations and combinations. Norman combines with Early English at Chichester ; with Decorated at St. Albans, Ely, Hereford, Southwell and Carlisle ; Perpendicular is thrown upon earlier styles at Worcester, Gloucester, Winchester and Ripon ; Early English stands almost alone at Salisbury and Southwark, and plays its part at Wells, along with Decorated and Perpendicular. And though in some of the buildings the Romanesque original is gone altogether, these are a minority. Not very often are we allowed to forget William the Conqueror ; like the eternal record of his Domesday Book, the architecture of his followers is the base and corner stone of all that comes after.

III

EARLY ENGLISH CATHEDRALS

AS we all know from the text-books, the great styles of English architecture each lasted for about a century ; and in each case the appearance of a fully mature style was introduced by about a half-century of transition. Simply as a rough approximation, easily remembered, we may say that Norman lasted from 1050 to 1150 ; Early English to 1250 ; Decorated to 1350 ; Perpendicular to 1450 ; Tudor to 1550. The famous Transitional style was that towards Gothic, in the period 1150 to 1200. It is true that even before 1150 there had been the first glimmers of a Gothic spirit in England. If we accept the view that the style first emerged as an entity at the abbey of St. Denis between 1132 and 1144, it is still true that all the three leading characteristics of the original Gothic, the pointed arch, the ribbed vault, and the flying buttress (though this last in a concealed form) had been built at Durham between 1128 and 1133 (3, 4). So that all the Gothic essentials were present in England well before the middle of the century.

It was again at Durham that the slender and aspiring quality of Gothic art was seen in the western Galilee, even though the use of round arches was maintained (47). But before that time, pointed arches were becoming general in the great churches of the Cistercians such as Fountains and Kirkstall Abbeys. Finally, the massive composition and structure of the Romanesque church began to be discarded, and masons of experience took daring risks in building thinner supports of better quality. Our first Gothic cathedral, in this new sense, took shape at Worcester, where the western bays of the nave survive (53). Although their exact date is unknown, they are certainly some few years earlier than 1175. Curiously mongrel in effect, these bays are yet our first Gothic composition. The clustering of narrow shafts, and the vertical emphasis which they give to triforium and clerestory, are a major landmark in style.

The bays are divided by shafts in series to carry the vault, a triplet flanked by an outside pair, making five attached rolls in all, running from base to capital, though interrupted by a moulding above the arcade. Even so, we have in embryo at Worcester the bay design of all the English cathedrals : a scheme which was even to provide the skeleton of Wren's St. Paul's. But there were still a number of subordinate round arches ; and within a few years these were to disappear.

The first all-pointed cathedral was Wells, completely rebuilt between 1174 and 1239. So important is Wells in the history of English Gothic that we should particularize its dates. All that is certainly known of this first Gothic building is that it was begun by Reginald de Bohun, who was bishop 1174-91, and who had already endowed the fabric fund for the purpose at a date before 1180. It seems reasonably certain that the choir was complete by 1192, and that the transept, nave (54), and north porch were finished, certainly before 1220, and probably by 1206. The great west front was then built, and finished before 1240.

Though small in scale, Wells is exquisitely proportioned. Its quality of workmanship is of the very highest, and perhaps nowhere are there so many foliage capitals of the first rank (55-60). The freshness of their carving and their immense variety are linked to a charming and genial humour, as where Farmer John is shown awakened by the sad news that " the grey goose is gone, and the fox is off to his den-oh " (55). It was perhaps unfortunate that the architect contented himself with the storied scheme of arcade, triforium and clerestory in separated bands, but the height of the clerestory and the groups of triple shafts clustering round the pillars do much to introduce the needed vertical element (52). The vaulting, with cross-arches and diagonal ribs, but no ridges, is of high pitch and suave curvature ; it is one of the most excellent in design of all our early vaults. The natural development from Wells would be to consider Christ Church Cathedral in Dublin, begun soon after 1172 and completed by about 1215. It was designed and built by Somerset men, and even with exported Somerset stone ; its resemblances are not only to Wells, but to the work at Glastonbury Abbey which began in 1185.

In another western cathedral, Hereford, some work of this period was going on, at the entrance to the Lady Chapel. But now came the first great importation of Gothic style direct from France : the rebuilding of the whole eastern arm at Canterbury (63-5). A disastrous fire in 1174 led to a conference of building masters, who disagreed in their proposals. The monks appointed one of the foreigners present, Master William of Sens, and the outcome was a plan and design markedly unlike the English type which we have seen developing. In some senses the new French Canterbury was a retrograde step ; the periapsidal plan and Corinthianesque columns of France were imported as they stood. And from comparison with Sens Cathedral, it is certain that Master William had indeed learnt his craft there. Sens was one of the earliest French Gothic cathedrals, mostly built in the twenty-five years from 1143 to 1168 ; it set a fashion which in France was adhered to throughout the early and classical period of the art. In England, fortunately, it was rapidly assimilated. This was partly due to the accident

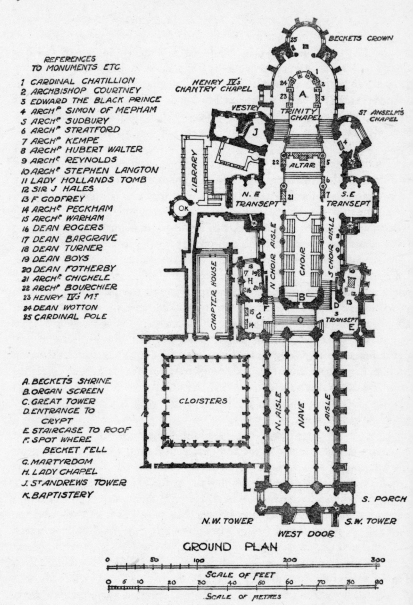

REFERENCES
TO MONUMENTS ETC

1 CARDINAL CHATILLION
2 ARCHBISHOP COURTNEY
3 EDWARD THE BLACK PRINCE
4 ARCHᴮ SIMON OF MEPHAM
5 ARCHᴮ SUDBURY
6 ARCHᴮ STRATFORD
7 ARCHᴮ KEMPE
8 ARCHᴮ HUBERT WALTER
9 ARCHᴮ REYNOLDS
10 ARCHᴮ STEPHEN LANGTON
11 LADY HOLLANDS TOMB
12 SIR J HALES
13 F GODFREY
14 ARCHᴮ PECKHAM
15 ARCHᴮ WARHAM
16 DEAN ROGERS
17 DEAN BARGRAVE
18 DEAN TURNER
19 DEAN BOYS
20 DEAN FOTHERBY
21 ARCHᴮ CHICHELE
22 ARCHᴮ BOURCHIER
23 HENRY IVᵗˢ Mᵀ
24 DEAN WOTTON
25 CARDINAL POLE

A. BECKET'S SHRINE
B. ORGAN SCREEN
C. GREAT TOWER
D. ENTRANCE TO CRYPT
E. STAIRCASE TO ROOF
F. SPOT WHERE BECKET FELL
G. MARTYRDOM
H. LADY CHAPEL
J. ST ANDREWS TOWER
K. BAPTISTERY

BECKETS CROWN
HENRY IVˢ CHANTRY CHAPEL
ST ANSELM'S CHAPEL
VESTRY
TRINITY CHAPEL
LIBRARY
ALTAR
N. E TRANSEPT
S. E TRANSEPT
N CHOIR AISLE
CHOIR
S CHOIR AISLE
CHAPTER HOUSE
TRANSEPT
CLOISTERS
N. AISLE
NAVE
S AISLE
S. PORCH
N. W. TOWER
WEST DOOR
S. W. TOWER

GROUND PLAN

SCALE OF FEET

SCALE OF METRES

Canterbury : the first greatly lengthened choir, with double transepts.

to William of Sens in 1178, which put control of the work into the hands of his English assistant, the second William. He rapidly developed his master's style and even in the strange Trinity Chapel and Becket's Crown imparted a certain national flavour, which a few years later was to be even stronger in the rebuilt retrochoir at Chichester (12).

But though indebted in certain details to Canterbury, Chichester was fundamentally English, with its square east end (66). And so was the other first class work of the outgoing century : Lincoln. Francis Bond carefully analyzed the features which Lincoln derived from Canterbury, and showed that with one exception, the buttresses, these features from Canterbury were not French, but English. But analysis is at best only a series of finger-posts ; it would hardly be possible for two great churches built in the same country almost at the same time to be less alike in feeling than are Canterbury (64) and Lincoln (68). And it is in this feeling, an atmosphere not definable by analysis, that Lincoln is so richly and fundamentally English. Even more, it is supremely Gothic, in a way that no French cathedral had yet been : precisely because it discarded the last remains of the Romanesque tradition in columns, capitals and bases. Bourges, the first fully emancipated French cathedral, was the exact contemporary of Lincoln.

At Lincoln we have the supreme type of the Early English cathedral. Not as exclusively of the one period as Salisbury, it is by this very fact more typical of English development. Yet its whole design, apart from the preserved Norman front, forms a complete scheme, differing only in details. The bay design adopted to start with was carried through in essentials to the finish (68, 93). And it is a bay design which, following on from the precedent of Worcester as much as from Canterbury, stands in the direct line of English development. Its one freakish eccentricity, the " staggered " vault-ribs of the choir, was quietly dropped in the later continuations.

Many years ago J. H. Parker showed that there was no real reason to suppose that Geoffrey du Noyer, recorded as " builder of the noble structure" (nobilis fabricae constructor), was a Frenchman imported by St. Hugh. The family of du Noyer were of Norman origin, but had been in Lincolnshire a hundred years before the building of Lincoln Cathedral, and long continued as a county family. But it is by no means certain that the description of du Noyer actually implies that he was the architect of the building. As so frequently happened in the accounts of architecture by mediaeval clerics, it may well be that Geoffrey was the administrative rather than the technical chief. And this tends to be borne out by Mr. J. W. F. Hill's recent discovery that during the last years of the twelfth century, one Master Richard the mason was holding land from the dean and chapter.

Nowhere better than at Lincoln can we see the aspiring quality of Gothic art. We must, of course, reconstruct in the mind's eye the three spires of which the minster has been robbed : the central one the highest work of man ever erected in this country. If we do this, we shall see that everything

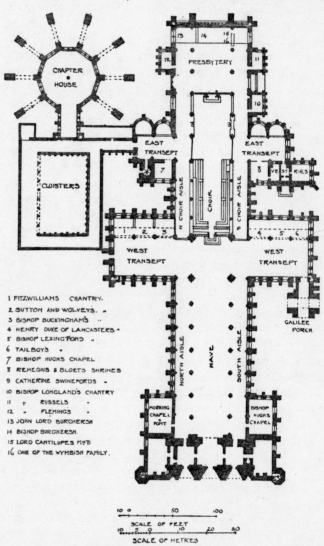

1 FITZWILLIAMS CHANTRY.
2 SUTTON AND WOLVEYS „
3 BISHOP BUCKINGHAMS „
4 HENRY DUKE OF LANCASTERS „
5 BISHOP LEXINGTONS „
6 TAILBOYS „
7 BISHOP HUGHS CHAPEL
8 REMEGIUS & BLOETS SHRINES
9 CATHERINE SWINEFORDS „
10 BISHOP LONGLAND'S CHANTRY
11 „ RUSSELS „
12 „ FLEMINGS „
13 JOHN LORD BURGHERSH
14 BISHOP BURGHERSH.
15 LORD CANTILUPES M⁰D
16 ONE OF THE WYMBISH FAMILY.

SCALE OF FEET
SCALE OF METRES

Lincoln : full height type with double transepts and the largest polygonal chapter-house.

is of one piece : the whole great church from east to west and north to south, the subsidiary chapels and the chapter-house, is beating against the sky with its spires, its spikes, its pinnacles. The lancet windows in the gables, the tall lights in the great tower, all are steadily and insistently surging up to heaven. And inside, the shafts, the vaults and the pale flames of the windows are doing the same. Sublime imagination of Master Geoffrey or of Master Richard, or of both together.

But Lincoln as first conceived by Master Richard (or by Geoffrey) was not fully English ; its eastern end was a most unusual compromise between the French chevet and the English love of straight lines. It had long canted sides, off which chapels opened. This chevet was destroyed after 1256, and the existing Angel Choir substituted for it (93). Earlier in the thirteenth century there had been another English feature instituted at Lincoln : the polygonal chapter-house (69). The first chapter-house built in England with a central plan was the circular one at Worcester, going back to the first half of the twelfth century. Unlike the two belonging to Cistercian houses at Margam and Dore, it had ten instead of twelve bays, and this peculiarity was copied at Lincoln. The majority of the later polygonal chapter-houses had eight sides, except Evesham and Hereford, which certainly copied Worcester, and Bridlington, which may have borrowed its ten sides from Lincoln. Not only does Lincoln resemble Worcester in number of sides, but in dimensions also : the 56 feet of Worcester are just exceeded by the 59 feet of Lincoln ; in both cases there is a stone ribbed vault resting on a central pillar ; in both cases there is a surrounding wall arcade.

These close likenesses cannot be fortuitous ; it is evident that the Lincoln work was directly inspired by Worcester, and was intended to surpass it in size, as in style. When we find that the master responsible at Lincoln bore the same name as one who had shortly before been at work at Worcester, the conclusion that he was the identical man is irresistible. The new work at the east end of Worcester Cathedral began in 1224, and the mason then employed is described as Master Alexander ; at Lincoln, within the period 1235-48 appears Alexander the mason, master of the work. And there is no doubt that the works of the Lincoln nave, chapter-house and the lower stage of the central tower belong to the years between 1220 and 1250.

Before the completion of Lincoln, another great eastern church, Peter-borough, had been triumphantly finished. Its western porch, inspired by the Norman arches of the Lincoln front, was pure Gothic (70). Nothing more than the suggestion of deep niches came from Lincoln, and the individuality of the design was carried so far as to make the central opening the smallest instead of the largest of the three. This might have resulted in a lack of balance, had not the crowning gables and pinnacled turrets been carefully adjusted to a different rhythm. Among our early Gothic works, the west front of Peterborough ranks very high indeed. Beneath the gables, it seems to have been set out within a double square, and its parts are disposed

according to simple proportions. There is also a successful optical adjust-
ment in the stages of the shafting, as the spaces between the string courses
and rows of annulets increase upwards.

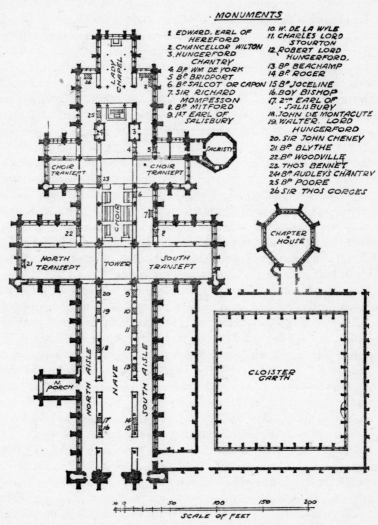

· MONUMENTS ·

1. EDWARD. EARL OF
   HEREFORD
2. CHANCELLOR WILTON
3. HUNGERFORD
   CHANTRY
4. B.P WM DE YORK
5. B.P BRIDPORT
6. B.P SALCOT OR CAPON
7. SIR RICHARD
   MOMPESSON
8. B.P MITFORD
9. 1.ST EARL OF
   SALISBURY

10. W. DE LA WYLE
11. CHARLES LORD
   STOURTON
12. ROBERT LORD
   HUNGERFORD.
13. B.P BEACHAMP
14. B.P ROGER
15 B.P JOCELINE
16. BOY BISHOP
17. 2.ND EARL OF
   · SALISBURY
18. JOHN DE MONTACUTE
19. WALTER. LORD
   HUNGERFORD
20. SIR JOHN CHENEY
21. B.P BLYTHE
22. B.P WOODVILLE
23. THOS BENNET
24 B.P AUDLEYS CHANTRY
25 B.P POORE
26 SIR THOS GORGES

Salisbury : the only cathedral of unified design, of "lower east end" type,
with double transepts.

Close to 1200 there was a period of great activity in the building of
fronts. In addition to the great porch at Peterborough, a Galilee was built
out beyond the western tower of Ely (42), an ambitious front was begun

at St. Albans, and from about 1220 work started on the sculptured display at Wells (71). The Ely porch was a long and narrow projection from the main wall, but both at St. Albans and at Wells the plan of flanking towers was adopted. Seen partly developed at Peterborough, this plan had been adopted for Rouen Cathedral in Normandy, still under English rule, and seems to have been a modification of the western transept found at Ely and at Bury St. Edmunds. At St. Albans the flanking towers were never completed, probably owing to the defalcations of Master Hugh Goldcliff, the original master mason, whose work collapsed during winter frosts. But at Wells the front was developed by Adam Lock into another triumph of English originality.

As at Peterborough, the Wells front was designed to fill a double square, but its internal organization was utterly different. The three aisles and two towers were marked by six buttresses of deep projection, and the extremes of the composition were taken up by the sides of similar buttresses facing north and south. Contrary to the precedent of the great three-porched fronts of France, and to that of the newly begun work at St. Albans, no stress was laid at Wells upon the entry to the church. The doorways are of very small scale, and hardly deserve to be called porches. Except for the main range of windows and blind niches, practically the whole area of the front is devoted to the display of sculpture, by far the most elaborate single display ever devised. Exactly what the iconographic scheme was, cannot now be recovered ; but it is at least certain that the complete work was as much a triumph of painting as of carving. Every statue was painted and gilt, and at its completion in 1242 it must have presented a dazzling sight, only comparable to the brilliance of the Parthenon in its first state. The front of Wells was the supreme triumph of the combined plastic arts in England. Henceforward the secondary arts were to be pressed into the background, though with advantage to architecture considered on its own merits.

While the first wave of Gothic cathedrals reached the west fronts, a new wave was beginning to rebuild eastern arms. This rebuilding took the form of extension, the new work being carried up around the existing Norman apses or fronts. This had partly a practical significance ; it allowed the existing sanctuary to be used for services continuously until the new was ready. But it also reflected a new emphasis laid on the sanctuary, eastern processional path and eastern chapels. Within the first quarter of the thirteenth century this transformation had been completed or at least begun at Lichfield, Rochester, Southwark, Winchester and Worcester. Of the masters responsible, only Alexander at Worcester is certainly known to us by name, and was probably identical, as we have seen, with the continuator of Lincoln. Peter des Roches, bishop of Winchester from 1204 to 1238, was the patron of the work at his own cathedral and of that at Southwark. Closely connected with the king's court, he may well have employed the Master Stephen who was the principal mason in the royal service at least from 1213 to 1228 and perhaps for a longer period.

But the great work of the time was the entirely new cathedral of Salisbury, begun when the city was removed two miles from the waterless mound of Old Sarum to the Avon valley. Salisbury is noteworthy as our only Gothic cathedral to be built on an absolutely unencumbered site. Its planning and design could proceed without reference to existing buildings or the necessity of maintaining services. To this the building owes its exceptional symmetry and regularity of layout, and also its eccentricities verging on preciosity. Within five years from the start in 1220 the Lady Chapel had been completed, and this set the keynote for the whole cathedral. Supported on grouped marble shafts of almost incredible attenuation, the Lady Chapel is of greater ingenuity than beauty (75). There is no reason to doubt that the king's clerk Elias of Dereham had a large share in this rather pedantic scheme, while the master mason Nicholas of Ely deserves special credit for the structural skill which overcame exceptional difficulties. Behind the eastern chapel the church grew apace from 1225 onwards, and by 1258 was completed except for the west front. The central tower and spire were not added until the next century, but the 38 years of the principal construction compare very closely with the 36 years of Wren's St. Paul's, our only other cathedral built in one operation. In both cases the full completion of the original project occupied about half a century. At Salisbury this included the building of very splendid cloisters (89) and chapter-house (90) by Master Richard, in imitation of those begun at Westminster Abbey. These were of Geometrical Decorated style, and belong to a later phase.

Before the arrival of Geometrical work with the new bar-tracery invented at Rheims between 1210 and 1240, there was an enormous burst of building activity in England. In addition to the works already discussed, there are extant buildings of the end of this period at Bristol, Carlisle, Durham, Ely, Exeter, Gloucester, Hereford, Lichfield, Oxford, Ripon, Rochester, Southwell and York. These include lateral Lady Chapels at Bristol and Oxford (76) and an eastern one at Hereford (78) ; north transepts at Lichfield and Rochester, and south transept at York (77) ; and chapter-houses at Exeter, Lichfield (18) and Oxford. Ripon built its version of the wide-spread west front, with triple doors between towers, and two tiers of five lancet windows (79). But the most important works were still concerned with the main eastern limbs of the cathedrals. Durham began its unusual eastern transept or Chapel of Nine Altars in 1242, under Master Richard of Farnham (82) ; Ely built its presbytery between 1239 and 1250 (84) ; and

Carlisle and Southwell were building their choirs (101, 102). It is uncertain whether the Durham eastern transept or that which so closely resembles it at Fountains Abbey is the earlier. But they resemble only each other, lofty and magnificent terminations of a type which did not become popular. Carlisle and Southwell were both under the influence of York, and were probably designed by York masons. The presbytery at Ely became the type of the Eastern regional termination, as Salisbury did of the Western. This regional diversity of design is all the more interesting in view of close resemblances of detail between the work at Ely and at Salisbury, which are probably explained by the Salisbury mason's origin or training at Ely.

By 1250 the Early English cathedrals had taken shape and were awaiting the next progression of style. In less than a century the whole country had put off the heavy mass of Norman building and accepted an entirely new architecture. True, it was in places bound by the plan and disposition of earlier work preserved of necessity, as for instance at St. Albans and Durham, but there was nowhere any doubt of the radical nature of the change. Already the interiors of churches were infinitely lighter ; in making comparisons it must always be remembered that our great Norman cathedrals, such as Peterborough and Norwich, have inserted later windows in place of those of Romanesque date. The gloom of a Norman cathedral must have approached that now only to be found in Mediterranean countries ; the early Gothic church, even where it is completely lit through rich glass as at Chartres, glows with light. But the disposition of the new windows was still not fully satisfactory.

Owing to the structural division of the Romanesque church into the three stages of pier arcade, triforium or blindstory, and clerestory, the architects were at first committed to a major difficulty which stood in the way of unity in design. In the relatively low English churches, there was insufficient room for all three storeys to be fully developed. If the arcades were to be even of adequate height, as at Lincoln (68), without unduly reducing the lighted clerestory, the triforium became too small. At Lincoln this was well managed, but the arcades were not high enough to give full effect internally to the vertical quality of Gothic art. At Salisbury the designer was determined not to fail in this respect, and produced tall arcades and exquisitely proportioned triple lancets in the clerestory, with a well-arranged vault. But in doing so he cramped the triforium arcade into positive ugliness, and also left it sitting on top of the spandrels of the arcade (83) in the same unfortunate way that had already occurred at Wells (54).

At Ely, the triforium is made the important stage, and is extremely beautiful, but the clerestory appears dwarfed, and the arcades do not occupy a sufficient proportion of the height (84). Even during the Transitional period an attempt had been made, at Oxford (46) and at Glastonbury Abbey, to eliminate the triforium by absorbing it into the main arcade. This was not a happy experiment, but it was followed by another which was to yield fruit. Before the end of the period a two-storey design had been adopted at a number of Cistercian abbeys, at Christ Church Cathedral in Dublin and at Southwell (102). In these cases the space of the triforium was absorbed into the design of the clerestory, to make only two stages of the interior elevation. The final and logical outcome, the bay of one stage only, was never fully attained in England, except at Bristol, by making the aisles the full height of the church. But it was hinted at in the stone grille applied to the choir at Gloucester (129, 135), and in the recession of the clerestory behind the plane of the main piers at Canterbury (146). The best solution of all could not be applied to monastic churches requiring a processional path, but was accepted at the Chapels Royal, where St. Stephen's in Westminster Palace and King's College Chapel, Cambridge, dispensed with aisles. This final result also appeared in Catalonia and at Albi in southern France ; it might well have been adopted for English cathedrals had a Catholic collegiate liturgy survived Henry VIII's anti-monastic reforms, and led to the building of a new series of great churches.

The best work of the Early English period has an incomparable fresh-ness, even where it forms part of a tentative and even ungainly design. It has the charm as well as the awkwardness of youth and immaturity : a coltish quality. Its finest flights were generally where the sculptor had free play, as in the leaf-capitals at Wells (55-60). It is certain that many of the early architects were themselves sculptors, and this was probably the rule. Only a sculptor could have devised the Wells west front as a gallery for figure-carvings ; a gallery of display so exclusively that the actual doorways look almost like afterthoughts (71). As the child is father to the man, so is Early English the progenitor of the whole of English Gothic architecture, and even of our non-Gothic building as well. It contains the seeds of all our later developments, though often lying dormant and hardly perceptible.

To consider the chief parts of the English cathedral, one by one, we can see the origins of future design in the bays, the vaults, the windows ; door-ways, fronts and steeples. As has just been mentioned, by the end of the period there were already bays which suppressed the triforium ; even at the very start in the nave of Worcester, there had been unity of bay design (53). Master Alexander's vaults at Lincoln included not only ridge-ribs (which had already appeared in Master Richard's choir vault) but even a system of short cross-ridges meeting lateral intermediate ribs which gave rise to the whole elaborate system of later lierne and stellar vaulting (68). In the contemporary chapter-house, the circuit of ridge-ribs between the central pillar and the walls even more definitely foreshadowed the lierne or strut-rib (69). Long before the actual introduction of Geometrical bar-tracery from France, it had been largely anticipated in effect by the ornamental piercings of spandrel which formed plate-tracery of considerable elaboration.

The main types of doorways had been formed before 1250. In the Ely Galilee, for instance, there was the door opening partly veiled by a central shaft and a screen of tracery (42, 86) ; at St. Albans were the English versions of the deep French porch ; at Wells and Salisbury were lateral porches highly typical of English tradition. Peterborough, St. Albans, Wells, Ripon and Lincoln were all producing versions of the wide spreading screen front, with or without lateral towers to flank the aisles. Salisbury continued the towerless tradition of Rochester. The narrow front with twin towers aligned on the aisles, a Norman design, was not favoured, but was to be adopted again at a later date. Central tower design suddenly leapt into prominence with the polygonal-buttress type at Lincoln (5), Oxford (85) and Chichester (66). These towers were based on earlier precedents, such as the Norman central tower with round corner turrets at Gloucester, but had become entirely Gothic. The lower stages of the existing tower at Lincoln, designed about 1238 by Master Alexander, led to the more important of the two great divisions of tower design. The other, based on the tower of Old St. Paul's built between 1200 and 1221, is seen only at Bristol (121), Durham (109), Wells (13) and York (140), and in hybrid form at Hereford (118), Gloucester (126) and Southwark (72).

Among subsidiary buildings the chapter-house takes first place, and is represented by the rectangular example at Exeter and the magnificent decagon of Master Alexander at Lincoln, where the form was already almost perfect. Only at Peterborough and Canterbury are there considerable remains of Early English cloisters, in both cases restricted to the wall arcading. But here too enough is left to show that there was a completed Gothic form, not merely distinct from the Norman work that had gone before, but already susceptible of individual variations. This individuality is indeed one of the strongest characteristics of the time ; there is no slavish copying, no adherence to sets of rules formulated by a man or a school. The vigour of Early English art is the vigour of English springtime, not confined to the regular blades of the young cornfields, but finding expression in an unending multitude of diverse forms.

IV

Decorated Cathedrals

THE Early English period in our art had been a brilliant and sunny spring; Perpendicular, as Sedding wrote, was to be the harvest-time of our endeavour, Tudor the fading glory of the autumn leaves. The period of swiftly-maturing development which intervened between the early and the complete Gothic was the full blossom of our architecture. Notwithstanding the fire of criticism which has been levelled at Rickman's term Decorated as a name for this style, it has a certain appropriate ring. For though there is much "Decorated" work that is restrained and even plain, the period does contain the peak of naturalistic carving and painting. Leaves, flowers and fruits, exactly copied from nature, and then richly stylized into undulations, run riot over the more costly work of the generations centred around 1300 (106-7).

There are, it is true, two great divisions within the style, separated by the introduction (about 1290) of the ogee curve : the Geometric and the Curvilinear sub-periods. In the first of these, designers struck simple arcs and circles with their compasses ; in the second, they joined their arcs into reverse curves and produced flowing, reticulated and flamboyant patterns. Foliage and natural forms are at first stiff, then towards the end of the Geometric period become intensely naturalistic, even photographic in their representation. In the Curvilinear style the crispness of natural leaves is lost, and the surfaces undulate more and more, producing strange nodules of rounded, globose form, connected by sweeping hollow surfaces which look as if they had been made with a vigorous thumb in moist clay. Before 1350 the quality of such work was becoming lush, decadent, and even repulsive to the eye.

Superficially, the patterns of Geometric bar-tracery in the windows and upon wall surfaces are the outstanding mark of the new style ; but they had far more than superficial importance. The introduction of bar-tracery meant another great lightening of the weight of stonework. Windows could be designed to consist mainly of glass, subdivided by very narrow mullions and bars, and supported largely by wrought-ironwork. This led directly to skeleton construction, where the weight and pressure from vaults and roof were concentrated upon a series of slender supports, and the intervening spaces of wall cut into window. This implied a further advance in structural

46

knowledge, and was accompanied by a greatly extended use of metal rein-forcement, which spread from the windows and arches into what was left of solid wall. Here was a revolution, tending towards the steel-frame building, the Crystal Palace, and all-glass solaria. At the same time, it translated into stone and iron the methods of the frame-wright who set up mediaeval timber houses.

Much of this revolution, at least of its origins, was accomplished inde-pendently in England, but the decisive features were a fresh introduction from France in 1245, when the new church of Westminster Abbey was designed. The foreign flavour of Westminster, its great height, its chevet, its grandiose north front, did not find favour in England. But the new windows from Rheims, and the renewed feeling of verticality, were rapidly made integral parts of the English cathedral. At Lincoln, between 1256 and 1280, the lengthened presbytery or Angel Choir was built in place of the curious chevet of St. Hugh (93). It adopted just so much as was essential from the new scheme of Westminster, including the angels which give it its name ; but in all respects it is a completely and even aggressively English building.

Similarly there is nothing French about the magnificent chapter-house (90, 94) and cloister (89) indulged in by the canons of Salisbury between 1263 and 1284. Unburdened with monastic buildings, these secular canons were able to finish in 21 years a work which at Westminster, even on a rather smaller scale, took 120. What is equally remarkable, the non-func-tional Salisbury cloisters are actually the largest, as well as the earliest, of the cathedral cloisters that remain. They may be considered as the starting-point of English cloister design, a highly specialized and interesting branch of our architecture. It became a point of honour to rebuild cloisters in the latest fashion, and much ingenuity was expended on them. Lincoln and Norwich (19–21) followed Salisbury's lead before the end of the thirteenth century ; in the fourteenth came Exeter, Old St. Paul's, Gloucester (127), Worcester (138), Durham and Canterbury. Peterborough, Wells, Oxford, Hereford, Chester, Ely and Bristol had all done likewise before the close of the Middle Ages.

The two great works of early Decorated are the Angel Choir at Lincoln (93) and the nave of Lichfield (98). At Lincoln, where the designer was probably a Yorkshireman, Master Simon " de Tresk " (Thirsk), the bold, broad northern scheme was adopted. The arches of the pier arcades are only just pointed ; the windows of the clerestory are so wide as to be almost startling. The work is tentative, but remarkably successful as an essay in a style only freshly arrived in the country. At Lichfield the dates of the building cannot be precisely determined, and it is consequently impossible to relate the different parts to the succession of masters : Thomas (*c.* 1230-50) ; his son William (*c.* 1250-65) ; and Thomas Wallace or the Welshman (*c.* 1265-80). It seems probable that Thomas the elder was architect of the transepts and chapter-house, and Thomas Wallace the designer of the west front and scheme of three towers ; William FitzThomas may have been responsible for the nave.

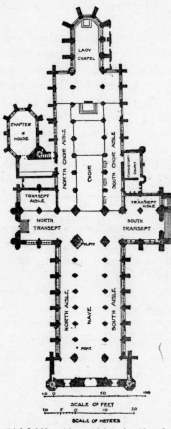

Lichfield : with apsidal Lady Chapel and polygonal chapter-house.

To whomsoever due, the Lichfield nave was another definite forward step in bay design. The arches are much sharper than at Lincoln, the triforium taller, while the clerestory has the beautiful and unusual feature of triangular windows formed of three equilateral arcs, and filled with three trefoil-cusped circles (98). From base to vault triple shafts rush upwards without a break, crossing a cinque-foiled circle which fills the spandrel between each pair of arches. As at Lincoln, there is arcading along the internal face of the aisle walls, and above this three-light windows with traceried heads of three cusped circles. The reduction of the clerestory windows to tracery alone, without vertical lights, couples them to the triforium beneath, and again suggests the two-storied interior. There is another, more freakish but less successful, version of the same design in the north transept at Hereford, which is roughly contemporary (118). This has arches composed of arcs of such large radius as to be almost straight lines, and an unpleasantly harsh effect of saw-teeth is produced.

All of this activity was taking place at the secular cathedrals, and marks the change of emphasis of the thirteenth century, abandoning the great abbeys for the bishop's churches. This reflected an actual loss of power and influence by the monastic orders. In the diocese of Bath and Wells, where effective power had been transferred to the abbey at Bath in 1090, it

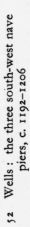

53 Worcester: the two Transitional bays at the west of the nave, c. 1170

52 Wells: the three south-west nave piers, c. 1192–1206

54   Wells : looking across the west end of the nave

55–60 Wells : variety of design in the foliated nave capitals

62 The south side of the Angel choir and its porch; 1256-80, by Simon of Thirsk

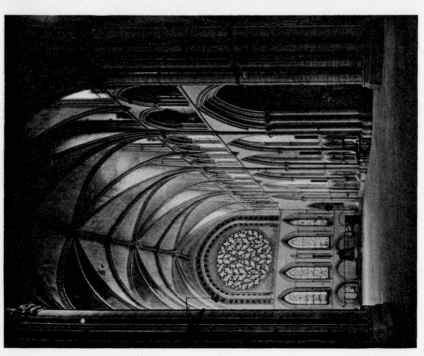

61 The south transept, c. 1200-20, with the "Bishop's Eye" rose window, perhaps by Master Michael

63   Canterbury : the eastern limb from the south-east, 1175–84

64 Canterbury: the choir, 1175–78. Designed by William
of Sens and William the Englishman

65 Canterbury : the choir apse ; 1179–84. Designed by
William of Sens and William the Englishman

66 Chichester from the south-east; 1187–99, tower
c. 1244–47, rebuilt 1861–66; original spire c. 1391–1402,
by John Mason

67   Chichester: the nave looking east;   1114–48, recased
1187–99, by Walter of Coventry

68   Lincoln nave looking east, c. 1225–53. Probably designed
by Master Alexander

69 Lincoln: the interior of the decagonal chapter-house,
c. 1220–35. Probably designed by Master Alexander

70 Peterborough: the west front, c. 1193-1220, with the
Perpendicular porch, c. 1375

71 Wells : the west front, c. 1220–39. Probably designed by Adam Lock

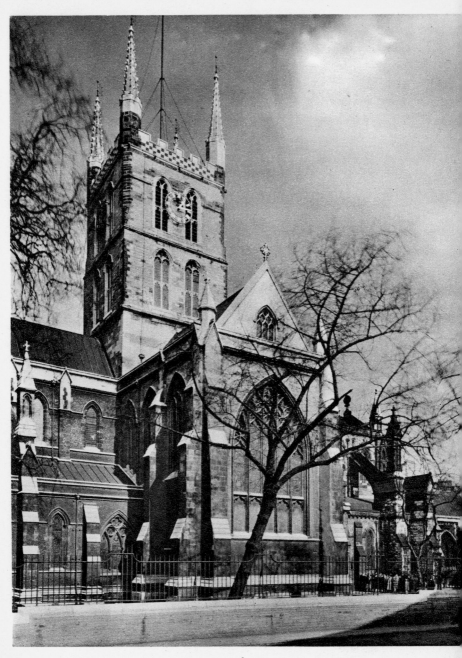

72 Southwark from the south. The tower, c. 1400, perhaps
designed by Henry Yevele

75 Salisbury: the Lady Chapel, 1220-25, designed by
Nicholas of Ely

76 Oxford : the Lady chapel, c. 1220–50, and the north choir aisle

77　York : part of the south transept, 1220–41, and the crossing

78 Hereford Lady chapel, c. 1220

80 The south side

81 The east end, c. 1288–97

79 The west front, c. 1230–40

RIPON

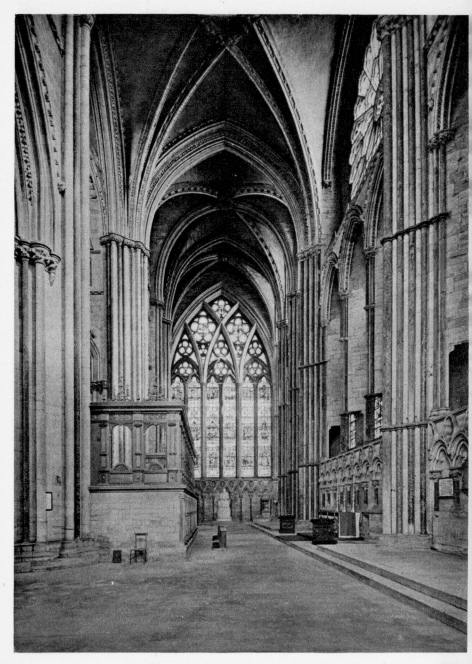

82　Durham: the Chapel of the Nine Altars; 1242–80, by Richard Farnham

83 Salisbury nave from the south west, 1237–58

84   Ely : the presbytery looking west, 1239–50

85   Oxford : the nave and south transept (1158–80) from the cloisters

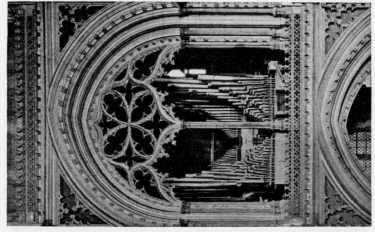

88　The choir triforium, c. 1330

87　The western doorway, c. 1200

86　A pier of the Octagon, with a scene from the life of St. Etheldreda on the capital; c. 1325, by Master John

89 **The cloisters, north and east ranges.** Both c. 1263–84, designed by Master Richard

90 The chapter house vault

SALISBURY

91 Chester : the refectory pulpit, early XIII century

92 St. Albans : the saint's shrine, c. 1302–08, and the watching loft

finally went back to the secular church of Wells in 1218. The abbey of Coventry, joint-cathedral with Lichfield of a great see, dropped more and more into the background. At Worcester, the bishops were so constantly at loggerheads with the monks that they withdrew to Westbury-on-Trym, near Bristol, and repeatedly tried to erect Westbury into a cathedral. The first of these efforts was made by Bishop Giffard towards the end of the thirteenth century, the age we are now considering. Another movement which was greatly lessening monastic influence was the spread of the orders of friars, introduced to England early in Henry III's reign, and generously fostered by him.

Work went on apace. Lichfield continued its nave and reached the west front (22), while York began its new nave (103) and Ripon an east front (81). Lady Chapels were built at Chichester (99) and St. Albans, chapter-houses of great splendour at Wells (100), York and Southwell (106). The Augustinian canons at Carlisle remodelled the choir after a destructive fire in 1292 (101), and Rochester built its south transept. But, apart from the work at York, by far the most important was the beginning of the total rebuilding of Exeter Cathedral (110-12), started in the eastern chapels at an uncertain date near 1280, and transformed into a scheme for a complete new church in 1288. Exeter and Bristol (122-4), which was not begun until ten or more years later, are our two complete Decorated cathedrals. Both, in their quite different ways, display the suavity and rounded qualities of the new style, now fully developed. The stiff, even hard crispness of Early English work has now altogether worn away, and everything speaks of the blown petal.

The approaching maturity of Gothic architecture in the later thirteenth century was shown not only in its decorative aspects, but in structure. A much larger proportion of the greater churches was intended from the start for high vaults. The building masters had proceeded beyond their tentative beginnings and had formulated a constructional system. Where before they had worked their way by guess and by God, they now piled stone on stone with well-founded confidence. Dissimilar in system as in detail as are Bristol and Exeter Cathedrals, in both can be seen this assured and well-rounded technique, free from the disproportions, as well as devoid of the naïve charm that had characterized the adolescent Early English. Exeter has a gracious generosity of form that typifies its Devon setting. Nothing is calculated to startle or astonish ; everything is soothing, but with a well-assorted and various charm. The tracery patterns of the windows are as appetising an assortment as a good box of chocolates (110). There is too perhaps a suspicion of the miniature perfection of bridal confectionery. This is one of the strange features of much Decorated work : that it seems less to have been built than to have been cast in a mould.

4

Old St. Paul's : the east end, 1251–c. 1300.

[From an engraving by W. Hollar

But the Exeter design unites beauties drawn from the examples of Lincoln and Wells, and carries a stage further the development of vaulting. Additional (*tierceron*) ribs are added to form a sheaf already approaching the fan in feeling (112). And though choir and nave were carried out according to the same scheme, the nave vault (111) represses the flattened curve of the diagonal ribs, introducing a refinement at the expense of " true " setting out. But this nave vault was not built until the middle of the fourteenth century, and such refinements in the interests of optical unity are really typical of Perpendicular Gothic. As in the Angel Choir at Lincoln (93), the Exeter arches are but slightly pointed, and so add to the broad and flowing qualities of repose which at Exeter are outstanding in the general impression. The new atmosphere of space and light is also noticeable, but there is not yet a fully satisfying resolution of the problem of bay design, and horizontal and vertical elements are too evenly balanced.

The chief connecting link between earlier and later, and eastern and western styles is lost : the new work of Old St. Paul's. This was in progress through the whole of the second half of the thirteenth century, and translated into almost aggressively English terms, the French Geometrical style. Its great eastern rose set above seven narrow lights (p. 50) was a counterpart to the bay design at Lichfield, where spherical triangles took the place of the rose (98). For some reason the rose never achieved a lasting popularity in England as an architectural form, though Paul's window was paraphrased on a smaller scale, and appeared as a design on tiles and elsewhere. The vault of this London work was provided with single pairs of tierceron ribs in each direction.

The building of Exeter was entirely finished in less than a century. Work began at the east end somewhere about 1275, with a Lady Chapel flanked by side chapels and backed by a retrochoir of one bay (110). Before these had been vaulted, the " new work " proper, the presbytery had been founded in 1288. It was complete in about twenty years, the master for at least the last eleven being one Roger, who may well have been the designer of the whole scheme. He was succeeded in 1310 by William Luve, under whom the church reached the first bay west of the crossing. At this period stalls were made under Master John of Glaston and a bishop's throne of wood to the design of Thomas of Winton (112). The next chief mason, Thomas of Witney, had charge from 1316 to 1342, and built the nave except for its vault, the high altar, sedilia and pulpitum, and eastern and northern cloisters.

It is an outstanding fact of the documentary history of Exeter that most of the principal craftsmen came from other counties. Master Thomas was presumably from the Witney in Oxfordshire ; the carpenter Thomas was from Winchester ; a master mason, William de Schoverville, from Salisbury, was called in in 1311. During the building of the western screen and the vaulting of the nave the masters were the two well-known Somerset men, William Joy and Richard Farleigh, and between 1376 and 1382 the cloisters were completed by Robert Lesyngham, a visiting architect from Gloucestershire, who also designed the new east window (110).

Within the century of its growth, at least five chief masters contributed to the development of Exeter, and yet they all adhered closely to the original concept of the first planner, who may have been Master Roger. The whole building is extremely regular and symmetrical, and embodies all the main characteristics of the age. Its eastern arm is built up on the lower surrounding chapels and eastern transepts, definitely a study in composition (110). The windows exhibit the ingenuity of the tracery designer ; the vaults show the increasing preoccupation with pattern and with suavity of line as an aid to unity. The nave is provided with the English lateral porch, but also with a western feature which was new. This was the separate screen containing three porches, and standing in advance of the main gable (133). It is an alternative to the cavernous porches of the French cathedrals, integrally planned as part of the front itself. The French scheme was to have been combined at St. Albans with the English lateral towers, but was never finished. At Lichfield and at Wells there were sculpture galleries on the fronts, but the doorways were not emphasized nor protected by porches (22, 71). At Exeter it seems to have been William Joy, fresh from Wells, who devised this new departure, but like the rest of his work, it belongs strictly to the story of Perpendicular architecture, and must be discussed later.

But the later Decorated period was one of lively experiment. Not only were the architects' compasses busy in the composition of tracery patterns ; great structural features were beginning to take on their final forms. Much of the underlying form of Perpendicular was present before its details started to appear in the fourth decade of the fourteenth century. Indeed, isolated details, not yet united in the Perpendicular manner, had been on view for nearly fifty years. The most noteworthy example of this tendency is the nave of York, begun in 1291 and finished, except for its timber vault, by 1345 (103). Of great width, with relatively slender piers, this design at the same time greatly increases vertical emphasis by its pronounced vault shafts which run unbroken from base to springing, and even more by its incorporation of the triforium into the clerestory. The triforium gallery actually consists of downward prolongations of the window mullions. So definitely does this design foreshadow Perpendicular treatment that it was possible to adhere to it very closely in the eastern arm built after 1350. The designer of this great work was apparently Master Simon, who was already a wealthy man in 1301, and died in 1322.

The new east front of Carlisle followed from the west front of York, and the breadth and space of the new idea were being simultaneously exploited by the king's masons in the south, where the immense church of the London Greyfriars was begun in 1306. The lantern church was fast taking shape : piers were being reduced to the smallest practicable cross-section ; windows were reaching their limits, as at Carlisle (101) ; and interiors were unified in treatment. The elimination of aisles was a logical step, but was not actually taken in any English cathedral. The architectural type, however, existed in the Chapel Royal of St. Stephen in the Palace of Westminster, begun in 1292, and followed by other chapels such as those of Eton College and King's College, Cambridge. Related to this aisleless scheme is the spacious eastern Lady Chapel at Lichfield, lit by very tall traceried windows (114-15). It was begun about 1310, and finished by 1336 ; the mason was William of Eyton.

Following upon the example of Salisbury, large cloisters were undertaken at several cathedrals : those at Lincoln were begun in 1296, and those of Norwich two years later (19-21). Here too was an atmosphere of space and light, as well as much ingenuity of design expended on buildings wholly or largely for show. But the great example of English architecture for show is the design of towers. Most of the famous towers are later works of the Perpendicular period, but their types derive from earlier models. As we have seen, there were two great schools of tower design : the turreted form derived from Lincoln, and the buttressed scheme found at Old St. Paul's. The upper stage of the Lincoln tower was built by Richard of Stow between 1306 and 1311, and ranks among the finest in the whole country (5). Standing on the low arcading of the Early English storey, it achieves its effect in one tall stage composed of two pedimented windows each of two lights. At Lichfield the central tower was to carry a stone spire, and was kept low, but it developed this theme by dividing the space between the turrets into five parts, of which two contained windows of two lights (22). The Lichfield turrets were buttressed at a lower level, and this two-stage buttressing was adapted to a non-turret tower at Hereford, built soon after 1320 (118). Hereford's tower is in two storeys, each of four panels, with twin buttresses at the angles, giving a somewhat turreted effect. At Wells a few years later William Joy built a tower of the turretless type, but quite unbuttressed, with three pairs of tall lancets on each face (13). This design was later complicated by the insertion of tracery in the lancets, and the addition of extra pinnacles. These four towers provided the elements from which all the later towers were to be derived by means of permutation and combination.

There was another experiment in a very different direction. This was the great octagon at Ely, built to replace the Norman central tower which fell in 1322 (108, 120). Following on the wave of polygonal chapter-houses.

the octagon presents obvious analogies to them. But it must also reflect some knowledge of the central plan abroad, and perhaps even of the great buildings of Persia, through the medium of travellers' tales. It is at any rate an astonishing achievement, with no direct parentage, and no immediate progeny. Among the English cathedrals only Wren's St. Paul's adopted this singularity of the Ely plan. We are told by the chronicler that the plan was devised by Alan of Walsingham, the sacrist, but the accounts record payment made to "a certain man coming from London to ordain the work", and show that the chief mason concerned was Master John. There is much plausibility in the suggestion that this was John of Ramsey, one of the important family of Norwich masons who were to lead the London fashion in architecture before the middle of the fourteenth century.

Original as the plan was, its scale proved to be beyond the mason's powers to vault. Nearly 70 feet in span, it also went far beyond the longest available timbers, and an entirely new method of construction had to be invented to cover it. This was the work of William of Hurley or Horley, who came from London for repeated visits, and was paid the very high retaining fee of £8 a year, worth something like £800 in the purchasing power of 1949. Although adapted to the octagonal plan, the wooden vault really consists of a series of hammer-beam trusses whose hammer-posts are the eight great uprights of the lantern (120). Though it had no direct results for the English cathedral, Hurley's adoption of the large-scale hammerbeam truss at Ely was to have far-reaching effects upon later English woodwork.

Concurrently with the octagon, three bays of the choir destroyed by the falling tower were rebuilt, between 1323 and 1336. Just as the Exeter vaulting was important for its introduction of additional tiercerons, so is the vault of this choir at Ely for its lierne ribs (119). The vaulting plan of the under-croft of St. Stephen's at Westminster was adopted, but with extra ribs inserted to form a series of six-pointed stars. This vault may be considered the progenitor, not only of the later lierne and fan vaults of England, but also of the stellar vaults which became fashionable in Germany and were among the chief characteristics of the central European "Sondergotik". The third work which was proceeding at Ely alongside the new octagon and choir was the Lady Chapel, a large separate building running parallel to the north side of the choir (113). Here, beneath a single span of vaulting, and enriched with sculptured wall arcades, is the embodiment of the spatial idea of later Gothic (117).

A different interpretation was put upon this idea at Bristol, where the choir, said to have been built between 1298 and 1340, is unique among English cathedrals as an example of the hall-church (121-4). The design is unusual in several ways. Not only are the three aisles of equal height, but the vault thrusts are brought down and equalized by a singular system of cross arches in the side aisles, supporting curious double vaults set sideways (123). This is structurally novel in England, and never was developed in that form. The piers too are a new version of the compound type, developed into a series of mouldings rather than a collection of shafts (124). The arcades have no capitals, but sweep up as a single series of mouldings from base to apex and down again to base. Here once more is a link with the methods of later German design, though this precedent was also followed in England to a limited extent. Finally, the central vault is formed with lierne ribs of another pattern, suggesting the netted complications of the retrochoir at Wells (125). There is in fact a close resemblance between these works, and together they form the vanguard of the Somerset-Bristol school of design.

We shall discuss the fourteenth-century building at Wells in more detail as forerunning Perpendicular. All that remains to be done here is to mention the final expressions of Decorated style in the English cathedrals. Centred rather to the north of the Bristol area was a local school characterized by the very lavish use of the ball-flower ornament. It is found in profusion at Hereford on the central tower (118), and in the south nave aisle built at Gloucester between 1318 and 1329 (128), as well as on the great tower of Salisbury begun about 1334 by Master Richard of Farleigh. There are indeed remarkably close likenesses of detail between the towers of Hereford and Salisbury (17), and also in the disposition of the windows in each stage. It may even be that Hereford, like Bath, Reading, Salisbury and Exeter, came within the scope of Richard Farleigh's skill. As a constructionalist he was outstanding, employing not only masonry flyers to spread the weight of the Salisbury steeple, but also hidden bands of wrought iron reinforcement.

Much of the building done during the period was of a tentative character : we have seen that several experiments had no progeny, at least in England. But this is not to say that they were fruitless. The full maturity of Gothic style in England was only reached after two centuries of constant endeavour ; and each and every experiment was of value. Certain steps were considered advantageous, repeated, and carried still further. Others were rejected, and the mistake, if mistake it were, was not repeated. And the benefit of these experiences was cumulative. We do not know exactly how they were stored up for use by the building masters, but arguing from the analogy of continental usage, we may suppose that each of the greater churches had a permanent masons' lodge and tracing-house, and that in the tracing-house was a collection of drawings. In no other way can we account for the nation-wide knowledge of past and current work possessed by the architects. Unprovided with printing or any means for the rapid and general dissemination of news as such, the building masters certainly had their own means of obtaining the information vital to their work. In some cases the fact of visits of inspection, or of the supervision of widely separated works by the same man, gives a precious clue to the course of events.

This spread and exchange of knowledge was general throughout England by the early years of the fourteenth century. Local ideas were, at least in the greater buildings, giving place to national ones. The same mason or carpenter might also be at work on an abbey, a secular cathedral, a private house, and the king's fortifications at one and the same time. No longer was art divided into almost hermetically sealed sections. There was an ebb and flow through all departments at once, a broader freedom and general interchange of ideas. This is certainly connected with the philosophic background of the new spaciousness and light of cathedrals and public buildings. The fourteenth century, like the nineteenth but with much better claim, can be termed an age of enlightenment and progress.

It has been claimed by eager upholders of the dimmer age of faith in the Romanesque and early Gothic periods, lovers of the religious light which was but darkness made visible, that our late Gothic cathedrals lack spirituality. This claim, which might have some grain of truth if it were confined to the tentative harshness of the choir of Gloucester (129, 135), or even the rather crude strength of York (103), has no general basis. There are no grander or more convincing monuments to belief in England than the naves of Canterbury (146) and Winchester (144) ; and it is only by reason of immaturity that the slightly earlier Decorated work falls short of the same standard. Judged, as they should be, by the standard of their own times, Exeter and Lichfield and Bristol are outstanding monuments of piety as well as of aesthetics. And in such extraordinary buildings as the octagon at Ely or the steeple of Salisbury we are raised by the alchemy of their creators to a higher plane of sensibility.

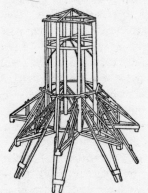

Framework of the Ely lantern.

[*From a model by Maurice C. Stubbs.*]

V

PERPENDICULAR CATHEDRALS

THE period of English architecture known as Perpendicular is really twice as long as the rest, for it includes not only the true style of the fourteenth and early fifteenth centuries, but also its later offshoot which is sometimes called Tudor. Since this last Gothic style was in fashion roughly for the century 1450-1550, while the Tudor dynasty reigned from 1485 to 1603, the name is unsatisfactory. Here, in view of the small total of buildings concerned, we shall consider a period of two hundred years in the one chapter.

It is our misfortune that we have no one complete cathedral dating from the best period of early Perpendicular. What we have to exhibit this maturest and most complete of styles is divided between half-a-dozen cathedrals haphazard. Without counting the tentative work at Gloucester (129, 135), there are the eastern arm and towers of York (134, 140); the central tower (145), part of the nave (143), north porch and cloisters at Worcester; nave (146), transepts, south-west tower (147), and cloisters of Canterbury; Winchester nave (144); and miscellanea at Norwich, Wells, Lincoln, Exeter and Chester. As is natural, considering the normal sequence of rebuilding from the east end, we are far richer in naves, porches, towers and cloisters than in sanctuaries or transepts. We have to go outside the cathedral group in search of comparable material, and even so find little of it, except at Bristol St. Mary Redcliffe, Christchurch Priory, and Great Malvern and Sherborne, though even these two last really belong to the later division of the period. It is only in St. Mary Redcliffe that we can savour to the full the spirit of unity which is the keynote of the style.

It is ironic that we should be unable to see a complete cathedral of that style which laid most stress on unity. The whole of Gothic development, and particularly in architecture in England, was working towards this end. The beautiful parts which to begin with were an end in themselves, had to be framed into an integrated, universal whole. The same movement which was at work in politics to produce the centralized and strong government of Edward I and the later Plantagenets, was also being applied to the plastic arts. The story of the progress of our architecture is the story of unification; its decline is written in a renewal of interest in the manifold parts of decorative pattern.

In considering the later Decorated cathedrals, we saw that the unifying tendency was already at work by 1290 or so ; significantly also the date of the first ogee curves. For while the separated circles of Geometric art lacked unity, it was the ogee that made possible the lively subordination of branching traceries. The ogee and unity of bay design, with the first symptoms of Perpendicular detail, arrived together. The essence of Perpendicular architecture is that the mullions of windows shall rush up to the arch itself without deflection, and that they shall actually meet or cut at right angles the horizontals in their path. This tendency has also been described as rectilinearity. So far as we know, the very earliest instances in the world of the mullion being carried straight up to the arch are in the great window of the south transept at Gloucester, whose reconstruction began in 1331 ; and in the windows of William Ramsey's Chapter House and surrounding cloister at Old St. Paul's, begun in 1332 (p. 60). Inasmuch as the side windows of the Gloucester transept show no sign of this characteristic feature, it may be doubted whether the design of the south window can date from the start of the work. If not, it was the metropolitan building, as might be expected, that first embodied the invention of the Perpendicular style.

But there had been examples of rectilinearity long before this. We have seen a trace of it in the triforium of the nave of York, begun in 1291 (103), and it was even more clearly marked in the choir of Guisborough Priory and the south nave clerestory at Bridlington, both in progress from about 1290. Similar solutions were roughly contemporary in France ; the York solution is close to the design adopted at Clermont Ferrand somewhere between 1262 and 1311 ; and almost the exact counterpart of the Bridlington triforium appears at Limoges in the choir begun in 1273 and completed in 1327. It may well be that England derived several of the basic ideas of Perpendicular from France, but it was only in England that they were ever brought together to form a complete style.

This style as seen in the cathedrals includes far more than the verticality of details which suggested its name. Its chief characteristic is the feeling of unity of space, no longer divided into bays longitudinally, into aisles transversely, or into stages vertically. The progressive thinning of the supports reduced the obstructions which had divided the total space into compartments. Refinements of detail, such as the vault-shafts which ran from base to springing in one line, and the union of triforium and clerestory, all tended to group the individual parts together. And now the proportions of the whole building were being studied, to give a total cohesion which could not be attained by the additive method of building on bay after bay to an indefinite number. The proportions of the exterior also were considered, and the massing of aisles against nave and of towers against the sky and grouped with each other, was the result of careful planning and modelling.

The reduction of the piers laid an emphasis on space ; that of the walls similarly stressed the access of light. Windows rapidly reached the limits of practicability, and at Gloucester the great east window was actually wider than the presbytery, being contained within a final bay whose sides were canted outwards to take it. Although the English cathedral remained low by French standards, its vertical lines were emphasized, and there was some actual increase in height over the Decorated norm. And in spite of the new emphasis on space, there was no abandonment of the linear qualities of English art, which were on the contrary increased. Vaults reached their limit in complicated patterns, and were then modified sufficiently to show their stellar or reticulated forms to the best advantage. Various devices were employed to increase the apparent height of the vault : thinning of the vault-ribs, as at Canterbury (146), and the use of pendants at Oxford (148). The spandrels over arches, both internally and externally, became filled with vertical panelling.

Many of the antecedent features which led to the new style had been brought together at the Royal Chapel of St. Stephen in Westminster Palace, where work on the main upper chapel started in 1331. William Ramsey, a mason of standing in Norwich, had worked at St. Stephen's at an earlier date, and was certainly familiar with the most up-to-date knowledge of the King's Masons and of the Canterbury School then leading the fashion. In 1332 he was appointed master for the new chapter-house and cloister to be immediately begun at St. Paul's. The design of his work can be reconstructed from an engraving by Hollar (p. 60), and from very considerable fragments recovered from the site in 1878. For the first time all the elements of Perpendicular were brought together, and the new style had arrived. It is important to realize that its origins had nothing whatever to do with the Black Death, so commonly invoked by those who would have us believe that the Perpendicular style is the product of penury and a shortage of skilled craftsmen.

Nothing could be further from the truth. The birth of Perpendicular was that of a genuine "new art", the result of long experiment and of the ingenuity of the greatest architects of the age. It was the style's misfortune to have been invented so shortly before a major cataclysm that its brilliant promise was partially enveloped in the great cloud of misery and fear. But there is no need to apologize for the best of the resulting works ; they are able to stand comparison with anything produced in England, or indeed elsewhere. The first of the cathedral works to be considered is the reconstruction of the choir of Gloucester, where the Norman structure was largely retained, but cloaked over with a screenwork of the new masonry (129, 135). After the south transept had been dealt with between 1331 and 1337 in an imperfect version of the new style, Gloucester immediately

Old St. Paul's: the Chapter-house and Cloisters, 1332– .

[*From an engraving by W. Hollar.*   [*Designed by W. Ramsey.*

proceeded to the transformation of the eastern arm between 1337 and 1350. The north transept followed in 1368-74, and the whole of the cloisters between 1357 and 1412 (127).

Coming at the very beginning of a period, the choir at Gloucester is a fantastic achievement. The gulf fixed between the mellow rounded effects of Exeter and this brilliant and clear-cut work of exactly contemporary date is immense. Far as Exeter had progressed along the road to Gothic fulfilment, its distance from Gloucester is not one hundred miles, but an age. Instead of accepting the existing division of the Norman church into three stages, the Gloucester architect cloaked the structure internally with a masonry grid, transforming the whole presbytery and choir into the semblance of an aisleless chapel. The aisles still existed behind the grille, but were not included in the spatial scheme. In other words, the procedure at Gloucester was the converse of that at Bristol. In the earlier work the central area was extended to embrace the whole church within the outer walls ; at Gloucester it was compressed, but in a translucent cage of stone and glass.

Gloucester is remarkable for the long continuance of its great building scheme. This was possible owing to the vast sums contributed by pilgrims to the tomb of Edward II (131). We may perhaps be thankful that the renewal of the nave proceeded no further than the west front and two adjoining bays, with a lateral porch (128) ; the grand Norman columns are in impressive contrast to the lofty and brilliant work east of the screen (35). But the rest of the buildings are all admirably in keeping with the choir, though their completion took over a century. The eastern Lady Chapel repeats the main motives of the choir on a smaller scale (130), while the central tower is a conversion of the Worcester design from the turreted to the buttressed type (126, 128). The cloisters with their early fan-vaulting are a new invention (127).

The style of Gloucester is so closely akin to that of the chapter-house at Old St. Paul's that we must suppose William Ramsey to have been the designer. From 1336 onwards, as King's Master Mason, he had the oversight of works at Gloucester Castle, and his wide fame is proved by the agreement of 1337 by which he agreed to visit Lichfield Cathedral to give his advice. There the Lady Chapel had just been completed, but had to be linked to the choir, which was on a different axis. Ramsey's presbytery compromises between the two alignments so skilfully that the breaks are not noticeable. He gave unity to the whole vista by rebuilding the choir windows to the same design as those of his presbytery, while retaining a simple tierceron vault design in keeping with that of the Lady Chapel. Vertical emphasis was provided by triple vaulting-shafts from base to springing without interruption.

Another type of incipient Perpendicular, more allied to the style of Bristol, was in progress at the retrochoir of Wells, where again an eastern Lady Chapel of the early fourteenth century (125) was linked to an existing choir. The work is of somewhat uncertain date, but was carried out under

William Joy, who also appears at Bath and at Exeter within the period 1330-50. The east window has two main mullions which cut the arch in Perpendicular fashion, and above the arcades and beneath the east window are vertical panellings forming nichework of great elaboration (132). Only the vault, a somewhat over-complicated attempt to improve upon that of Bristol, falls short of complete success. Joy's work also included the great central tower in its original form (13), and a few years later the unusual " St. Andrew's arches " by which it is propped up. Here, as at Salisbury, the tower was added to a crossing whose piers had never been intended for such a weight.

The beginning of the western screen and porches at Exeter about 1346 seems to have been another work by Joy, and its rich array of statuary may well have been inspired by the front of Wells (133). In type it was totally different, having only shallow buttresses and sheltering the doors behind porches with face-arches on the sculpture plane. But though on a much smaller scale, it does resemble Wells in ending on a horizontal line across the whole width of the church and aisles. The porches, though small, are of special interest, as they are the earliest examples of the typical Perpendicular " welcoming " porch, seen at its best in the west fronts of Winchester and Canterbury Cathedrals, Westminster Abbey, and the north entry of Westminster Hall. In a reduced form it also appears later at Gloucester, Norwich, Bath, and formerly at Southwark.

The west front of Winchester is a puzzling work, rather crude and unformed, yet characteristically Perpendicular (40). The type features perhaps make an even too obtrusive appearance. It is certain that the standard west front with twin towers was disliked by our later Gothic designers. Even at York, where it had been adopted at the end of the thirteenth century, the front itself was finished off on a horizontal line, behind which the towers stand as if planted on top of a box (134). Salisbury had followed the much earlier example of Rochester in avoiding western towers altogether ; so, later, did Exeter and Bath. At Gloucester and at Norwich, where Norman towers probably existed, they were carefully removed, and this certainly happened at Winchester. Everywhere, except at Exeter, the attempt of the designers seems to have been to emphasize the central nave by building flanking turrets, and to minimize the aisles. This front has been termed parochial, but it is hardly likely that the architects of cathedrals and great minsters would be so strongly influenced by the least significant type of parish church. It seems far more probable that what was attempted was, as in the choir of Gloucester, an innovation based upon the turreted Chapel Royal, initiated at St. Stephen's and found also at Eton and King's College, Cambridge, and St. George's Chapel in Windsor Castle.

If this view is correct, the " welcoming " porch is a reminiscence of the entrance vestibule of St. Stephen's Chapel.

How much of the Winchester front was built in the time of Bishop Edingdon is uncertain, but his will, made in 1366, clearly states that he had already begun work on it. Considering the resemblances of the porches and west window to Gloucester choir, there seems no reason to dispute Willis's conclusion that the main scheme of the front belongs to Edingdon's time. But the heightening of the end walls of the aisles, the gable, and perhaps the parapets, are later additions of Wykeham's time from the designs of William Wynford. The main work of the Winchester nave, not begun until 1394, will be discussed later.

At York the Lady Chapel was begun in 1361, and the master was probably Robert Patrington. The four easternmost bays were completed in twelve years, and the remaining five bays to the crossing were added between 1380 and 1405 to a different design by Hugh Hedon (141). In both cases the main lines of the original scheme laid down in the nave were adhered to, while the great east window closely followed the example of Gloucester, though with only nine lights instead of fourteen. The great triumph of York, its immense lantern tower, was to come later (140). This was the only English tower (unless the octagon of Ely be included) which is broad enough to be completely satisfactory from within. But, unlike the rest of the Minster, it was not built by a northern mason, but by William Colchester from Westminster Abbey, a pupil of Henry Yevele.

Also connected with the Court School of masons was the architect of the fourteenth century building at Worcester. Within little more than a generation, some thirty years following 1365, the church was brought up to date with a new central tower, south nave arcade, nave vaults (143) and lateral porch, and a complete cloister. It is probable that all this work was designed by the Master John Clyve who was in charge in 1376 and who had taken on several contracts at Windsor Castle from 1362 to 1365. The importance of his work is seen in the beautifully modulated cloisters (138), where (in part) the shafts branch out into vault-ribs by a sort of natural fission, devoid of capitals ; and in the magnificent central tower (145). This tower has strong claims to be regarded as the finest individual tower design of the whole Gothic period in England. Its proportions are exquisite, and it blends in the happiest manner the turreted with the buttressed form. The contrast between the vertical panelling of the lower stage and the windowed scheme above is admirably managed, and its scale is perfectly in keeping with the bulk of the church below.

Lesser works of the closing fourteenth century were the western towers at Lincoln, of c. 1370-80 (5) ; and the cloisters at Durham, begun in 1390 by John Lewyn and continued early in the next century by Thomas Mapilton. Lewyn had earlier vaulted the monastic kitchen about 1366 with an astonishing stellar polygon which recalls the Saracenic brick vaults of Persia (p. 68). He was a great builder of castles in addition to his work for the bishop and monastery of Durham. Mapilton was later to become King's Master Mason, and to design the south-west tower of Canterbury Cathedral, built between 1423 and 1434. In speaking of work of first-class importance, such as almost the whole of our cathedral output is, it is no longer possible to speak of local schools. Communications in the later fourteenth century were excellent, and the greater architects were moving from end to end of the kingdom.

Among these great masons, the greatest were two of those in the royal service : Henry Yevele and William Wynford. Born some twenty to thirty years before the great pestilence, they were able to seize the opportunity afforded by the ensuing shortage of artists. The essentials of the Perpendicular style had been laid down by William Ramsey before his death in 1349, and were being exploited in the years immediately following by successors such as John Sponlee, the chief mason at Windsor Castle. When Yevele became King's Master Mason in 1360 he was able to diffuse throughout the country, by means of the official buildings under his control, a perfected version of the newly achieved national style. Lasting for forty years, his term of office included the period of highest achievement in the whole history of English art.

Slightly Yevele's junior, William Wynford appears at Windsor Castle in 1360, and soon became joint master with the ageing Sponlee. Later he was to assume full control on Sponlee's retirement. Both Yevele and Wynford were employed by the king, but Wynford's especial patron was William of Wykeham, for a time clerk of the works at Windsor, and then provost of Wells and bishop of Winchester. Through his patronage Wynford found opportunities second only to those of Yevele. Appointed consultant master at Wells in 1365, he designed the western towers, of which the southern was actually built under his supervision. Here he showed his ability to design in harmony with earlier work, and to complete an existing composition in such a way as to raise it to a higher power. In this talent he followed the example set by Richard Farleigh at Salisbury and John Clyve at Worcester.

More important even than his work at Wells were Wynford's two colleges built for his patron at Oxford and Winchester. But we must here consider him as the architect of the nave of Winchester Cathedral, begun in 1394 and left in his charge at Wykeham's death ten years later. Although not finally completed until many years after Wynford's death, he was the designer of

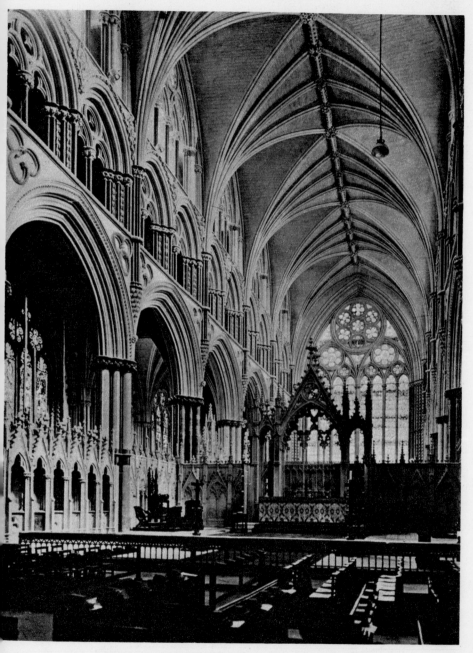

93 Lincoln: the Angel Choir, 1256–80. Probably designed
by Master Simon of Thirsk

94 The central west door, c. 1260

95 The chapter-house doorway

96 The chapter-house arcading, c. 1270

SALISBURY Detail

97 Ripon choir, looking east; c. 1154–81, east end c. 1288–97

98 Lichfield nave from the south-west; c. 1250–80, possibly
designed by William Fitzthomas

99　Chichester : the Lady chapel, c. 1288–1304

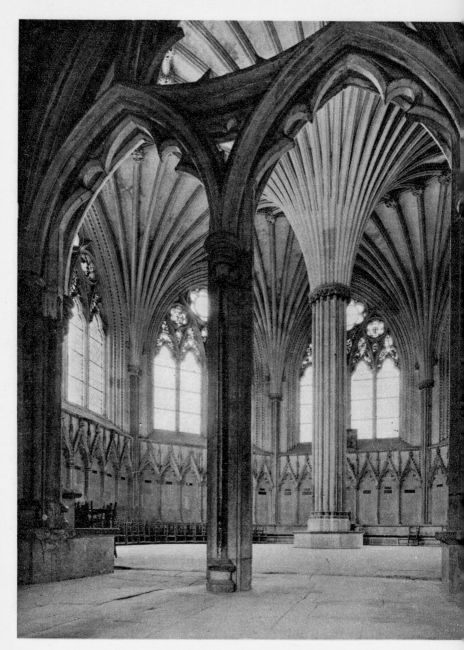

100   Wells : the chapter-house, c. 1293–1319

101 Carlisle choir, looking east; c. 1245–92, piers and east
bay 1293–1322, clerestory c. 1353–95

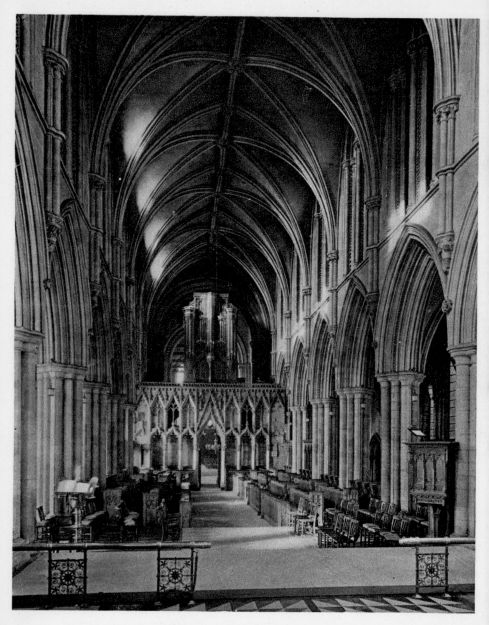

102   Southwell choir looking west to the screen; c. 1230–50, screen c. 1330

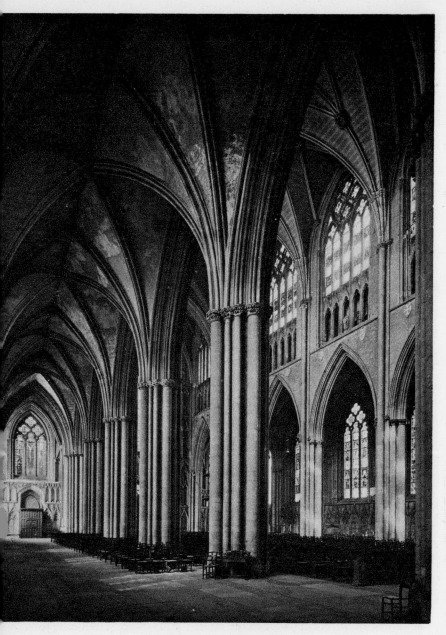

103　York: the nave from the south aisie; 1291–1345,
probably designed by Master Simon

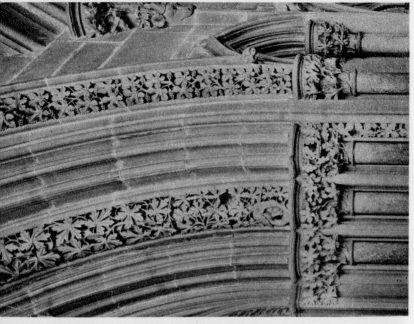

106   The screen, east side   107   The chapter-house door

SOUTHWELL Carved Detail, c. 1293–1300

109 Durham : the central tower (1465–90) and north transept

108 Ely : the Octagon, 1322–46, designed by "Master John," probably John of Ramsey

110   Exeter : the east end from the south ; c. 1275–1308

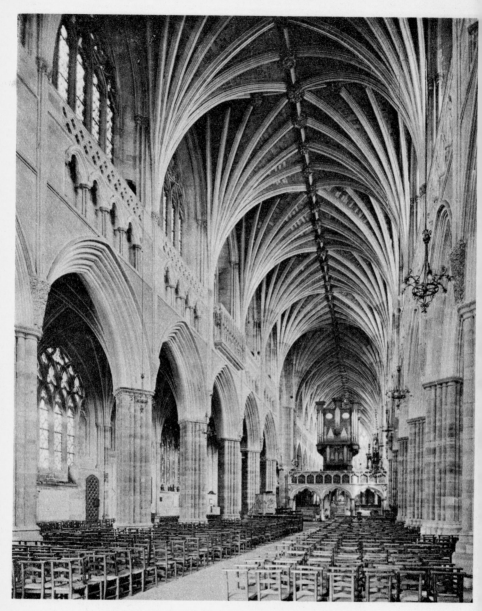

111   Exeter nave looking east, 1328–42. Mostly designed by
Thomas of Witney. The vault by William Joy and
Richard Farleigh

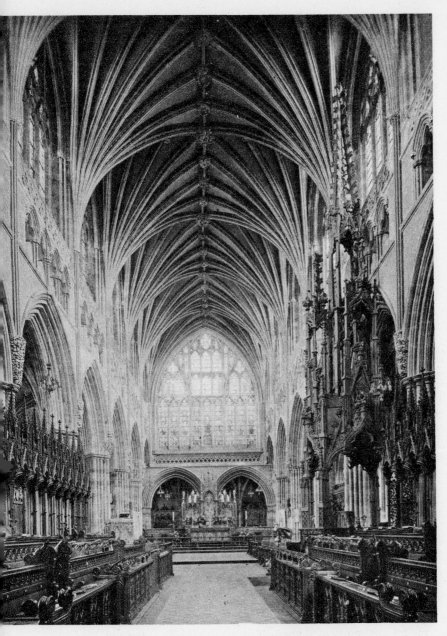

112 Exeter choir, 1288–1308, with the bishop's throne,
1309–17. The choir probably designed by Master Roger,
the throne by Thomas of Winton

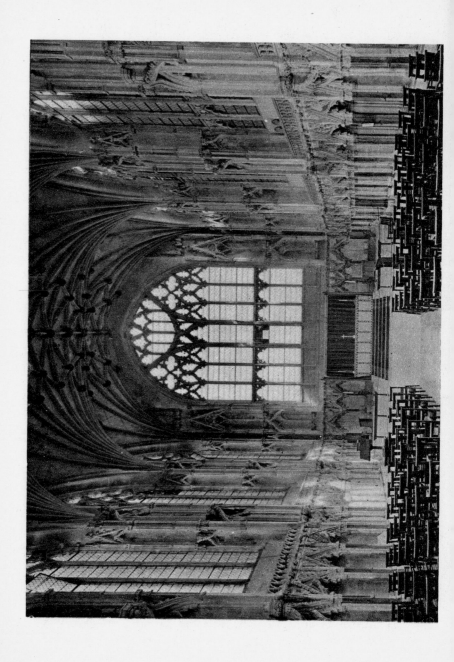

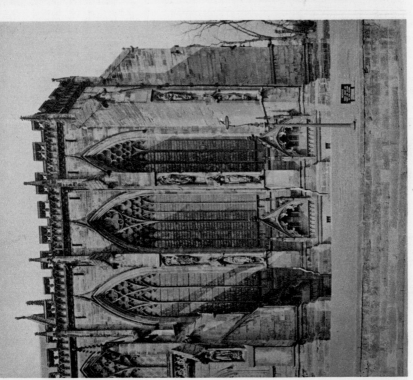

114–5 Lichfield Lady chapel: the south side and apse;
c. 1320–36, designed by William of Eyton

116   Lichfield : the interior of the Lady chapel ; c. 1320–36, designed by William of Eyton

117 Ely Lady chapel : detail of the arcading, c. 1330

118   Hereford: the tower, c. 1325, north transept, c. 1250–68, and Bishop Booth's porch, c. 1520–30

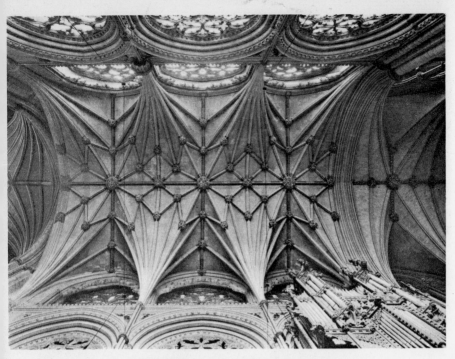

119 The lierne vault of the choir, c. 1335

120 The Octagon vault; 1328–40, designed
by William Hurley

ELY

121   Bristol choir from the south, c. 1311–40

123   The vaulting of the south choir aisle,
c. 1330–40

122   The north transept, crossing and
screen, c. 1428–73

BRISTOL

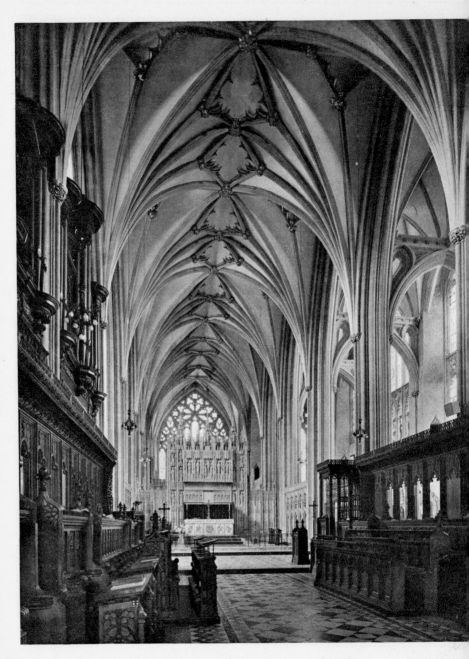

124   Bristol choir looking east, c. 1311–40

125 Wells Lady chapel from the retrochoir; c. 1293–1319

126 Gloucester from the south-east, showing the choir,
[...] d [...] In chapel [...] &c

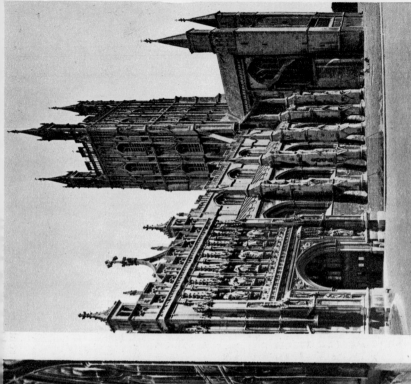

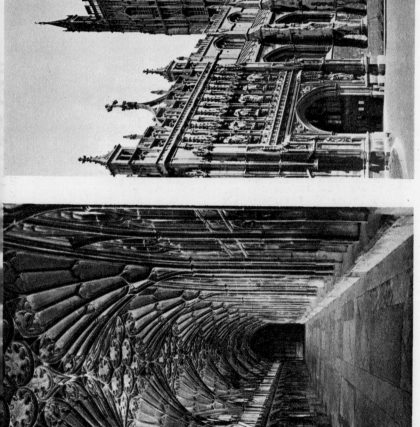

127   The south range of the cloisters, 1381–1412, possibly by Robert Leysingham

128   The south aisle, 1318–29, and porch, 1421–37

GLOUCESTER

129　Gloucester choir, 1337–50, probably designed by William Ramsey

130 Gloucester Lady chapel, c. 1457–83, possibly designed by John Hobbs

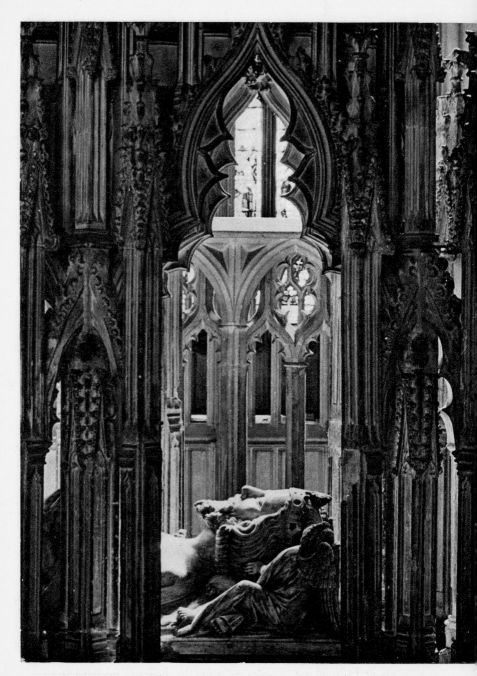

131   Gloucester : the tomb of Edward II, c. 1330, altered XIX century

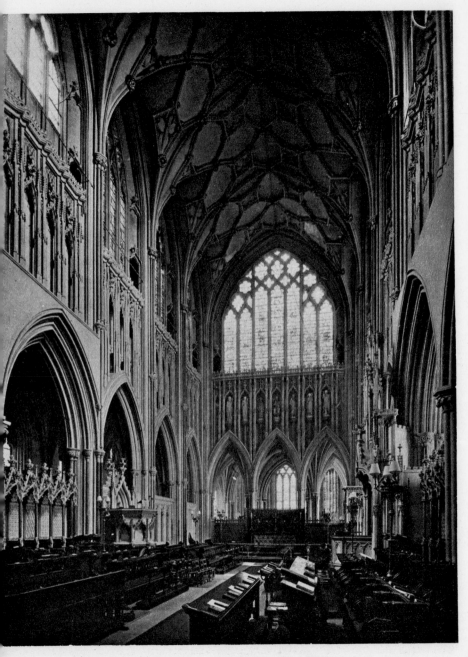

132　Wells choir looking east.　Reconstituted by William Joy, c. 1329

133 Exeter west front, 1346–75, in part designed by William Joy

134   York west front, 1291–1345 ; towers 1432–74, designed by Thomas Pak

135 Winchester: the choir, c. 1320–60, and
reredos, c. 1475–80

136 Gloucester: detail of the Perpendicular
casing of the choir, 1337–50

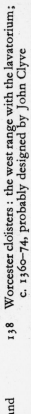

138   Worcester cloisters : the west range with the lavatorium ;
      c. 1360–74, probably designed by John Clyve

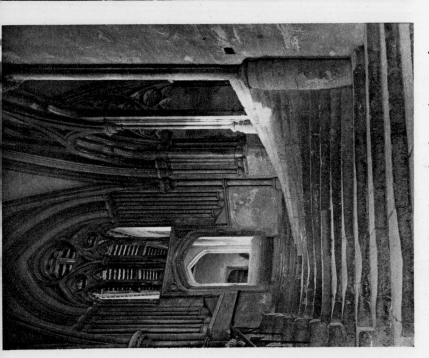

137   Wells : the stairs to the chapter-house and
      bridge to the Vicars' close

139   Chester from the north, showing the chapter-house

140   York : the south side.   The central tower, 1407–23, by William Colchester

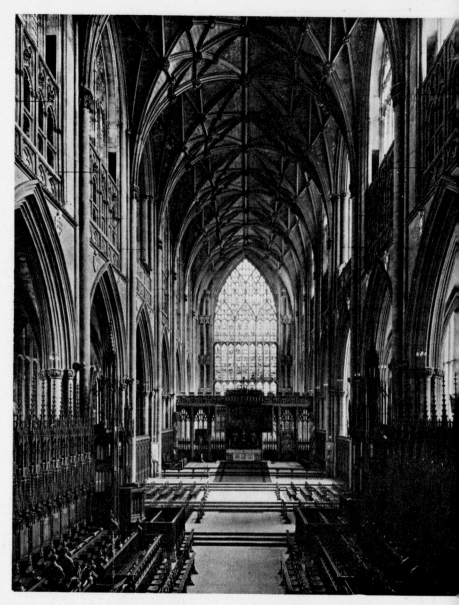

141 York: the choir, 1380–1400, looking to the Lady chapel,
1361–73, probably by Robert Patrington; choir by
Hugh Hedon

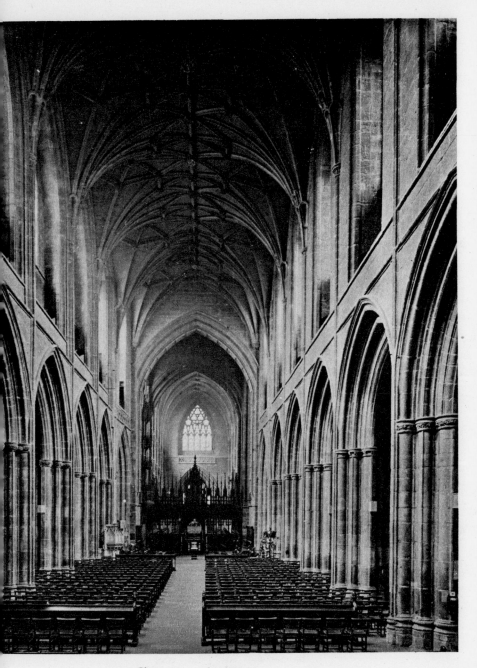

142   Chester nave looking east ; c. 1323–1492

143 Worcester nave looking east; 1317–74, by William Shockerwick and John Clyve

144 Winchester nave looking west; 1394–1450. Designed
by William Wynford

145 Worcester from the south-west across the Severn. The
tower probably designed by John Clyve ; c. 1360–74

146 Canterbury nave ,from the south-west ; 1379–1405, designed by Henry Yevele

147 Canterbury from the south-west. The nave designed by
Henry Yevele. The south-west tower by Thomas Mapilton,
the central tower by John Wastell. *Circa* 17

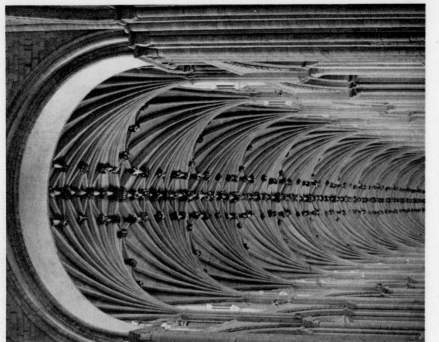

149　Norwich: the lierne nave vault; c. 1463–72, possibly by John Everard

148　Oxford choir: detail of the arcade and later vault, c. 1478–1503, possibly by William Orchard

150   The west front

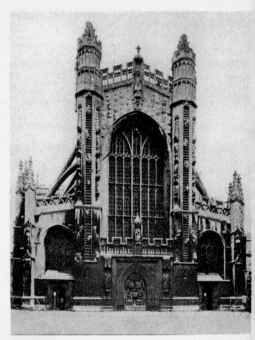

151   From the south-west

BATH, 1501–39.   Designed by Robert and William Vertue

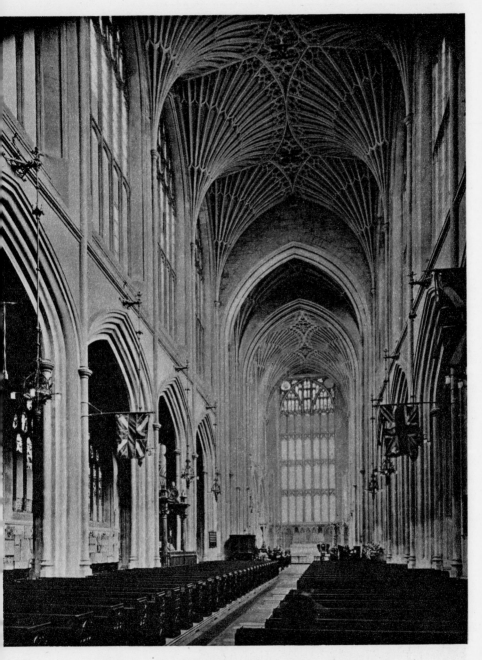

152   Bath : the nave looking to the choir.   Designed by
Robert and William Vertue

Winchester: the Beaufort and Waynflete chantries; XVth century

153 Peterborough: the fan-vaulted retrochoir; c. 1496–1508, by John Wastell

155 Bishop Alcock's chapel; c. 1486–1500, possibly by Adam Lord

156 Bishop West's chapel, 1534

ELY

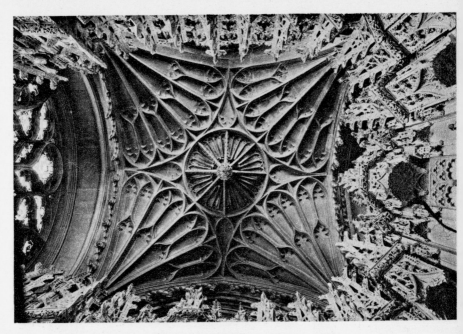

157   The vault of Bishop Alcock's chapel

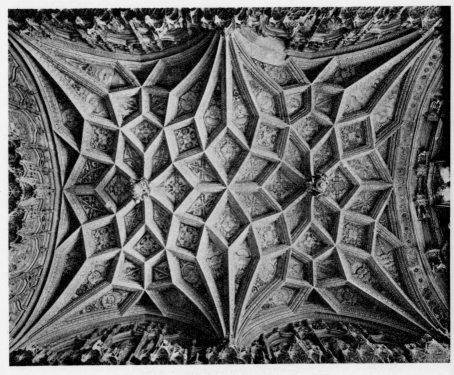

158   The Renaissance ceiling of Bishop
West's chapel

ELY

159   Bishop Waynflete, c. 1485

160   William of Wykeham, c. 1395

WINCHESTER Chantry Vaults

161   Canterbury : Bell Harry tower from Butchery Row,
1490–97, designed by John Wastell

162   Ripon nave; 1502-22, designed by Christopher Scune

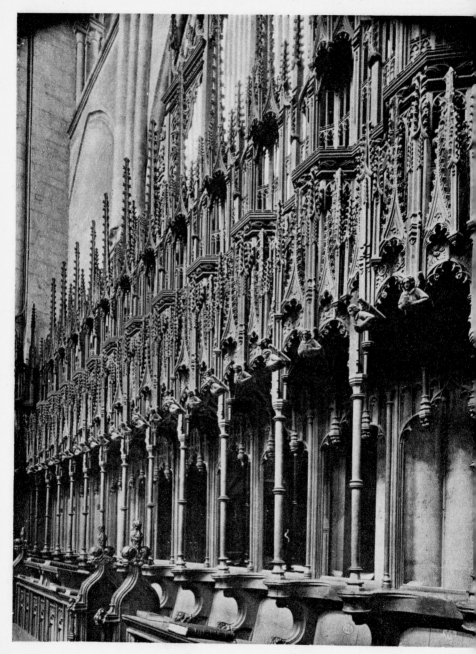

163 Ripon: the choir stalls; 1489–94, designed by
William Brownfleet of Ripon

164 Chester : the choir stalls, c. 1390

165   Effigies of Henry IV and Joan of Navarre,
c. 1415, probably by Thomas Prentys and
Robert Sutton

166   The effigy of the Black Prince; c. 1377,
probably by John Orchard

CANTERBURY

the whole work, apart from the earlier sections of the west front. Like Gloucester, the work was an attempt to alter without demolishing a Norman structure (144). But the two works were carried out by totally different methods. At Gloucester the inner faces of the Norman choir piers were pared off, and a skin of masonry applied as an inner cage (129, 135). At Winchester the old work was at first cut down and worked to new mouldings all round, and later cut out and refaced with new stones. At Gloucester the Perpendicular building is mostly but skin-deep ; from the other side, the original work appears unaltered. At Winchester almost everything was changed, and the very arches were replaced by others of a different form.

Yevele's methods were different again. Between 1375 and his death in 1400 he carried on the nave of Westminster Abbey, an adaptation of the early Decorated design of the choir. This was a new building on new foundations ; the Norman nave was first utterly destroyed. The same process was adopted at his great cathedral work, the nave of Canterbury. Before the pulling down of the old nave, aisle walls were built, beginning in 1378. After this there was a pause in the work, which was resumed in 1391. The design of the central arcade and clerestory, which differ in detail from the aisles, therefore belongs to that wonderful period around 1390. The moment was doubly fortunate : Richard II had just freed himself from the rule of the Appellants, surrounded himself with men of culture, and installed Geoffrey Chaucer as clerk of the royal works. And Yevele, his chief mason, aged about seventy, had reached the final maturity of his powers, and could produce a design so mellow, so unassumingly perfect, that its perfection passes unnoticed.

For the nave of Canterbury Cathedral is the supreme triumph of English architecture, which is to say, of English art (146). Completed after Yevele's death by his pupils and successors, Stephen Lote and Thomas Mapilton, the metropolitan cathedral became the exemplar of our own particular Gothic. And that it is so is because Yevele's genius was big enough to break the rules of development which were becoming fixed in his time. We have seen the growth of the towerless but turreted west front, and the tendency to minimize the side aisles : Canterbury on the contrary has tall aisles and a twin-towered front which, though not built by Yevele, was planned by him. And we can see how this movement against the tide happened.

Mr. Arthur Oswald has shown the very close resemblances between the naves of Canterbury and Westminster, and there can be no doubt that experience at Westminster was the decisive factor in Yevele's design. Canterbury, still the church of a great Benedictine monastery, must have aisles ; if they were low, according to the fashion, brilliant side-lighting

5

would be impossible. It would not do to split the total height into two equal parts ; and so the aisles became very tall indeed, gaining much of the effect of Bristol without suppressing the clerestory altogether (147). The clerestory windows were still of importance, for beside traditional value, they threw direct daylight upon the vault of the central nave. But with so tall an arcade, something must be done to prevent the piers seeming to be disconnected and wavering ; and the answer lay in the horizontal line of mouldings above the arches. This gives direction and at the same time brings together the whole arcade as one. So far as the limitations of the aisled scheme permit, the nave of Canterbury at last achieves the unity which the Gothic builders had been seeking for two hundred years.

Winchester, arrived at in a different way, and limited by the preservation of the Norman core, is hardly the equal of Canterbury, but it has the merit of providing an exactly contemporary solution that is altogether different. Instead of attempting the attenuated and brilliant glass house church, Winchester accepts the primitive sturdiness of its enormous piers, clothes them in the mouldings and details of the day, and sets above them a magnificently original vault (144). This vault with its upward leap is unlike that of any other cathedral, and seems only to be like the sweeping boughs of the beech trees on the neighbouring chalk downs.

After Winchester, the age of cathedral building was over. Within the limits of conservative English tradition, the last word had been said, and just as the monasteries had lost ground to the bishops, so the bishops were being ousted as art patrons by lay courtiers founding new colleges of secular clergy. The wheel was sweeping round full circle. On the whole it seems fortunate that little remained to be done, and that there was little money available. For the work that was carried out in the fifteenth century was rarely on the level of what had been accomplished by Yevele and Wynford. James Wodrove's west and north cloisters at Norwich (21) are outstanding exceptions. There is a good deal of pleasant but uninspired work at Chester (139, 142), and additions at other cathedrals such as the cloisters of Wells, Chichester and Hereford. The one field of design in which outstanding things were still being done was the tower : York (140), Durham (109), and finally Canterbury (147, 161) were supplied with central towers of absolutely the first rank, and interesting experiments were made at Bristol, Chester and Bath.

Towards the end of the century there was a revival, and Norwich vaulted first its nave (c. 1463-72) (149) and then its presbytery (c. 1472-99) (14). These vaults, of stellar lierne pattern, and approaching the fan-vault in feeling, are also among the finest in the country ; they culminated in the exquisite pendant vault of the Oxford choir (148). At the extreme east end of

Ely two bishops made exquisitely carved chantry chapels : that of John Alcock (*c.* 1488-1500) (155, 157), and that of Nicholas West, about 1534, already mixed with Renaissance details (156, 158). At Peterborough a more ambitious work was carried out between 1496 and 1508 : the New Work or eastern chapels surrounding the Norman apse (153), built and fan-vaulted by way of model for John Wastell's work at King's College Chapel, Cambridge. At Rochester the Lady Chapel of about 1512 was intended to have fan-vaults, but they were never built.

These last works are Tudor rather than Perpendicular in the strict sense. All of them are enriched with surface decoration of a repetitive kind, much of it curvilinear or even flamboyant in character. Decorative crestings and scrolls of leaves and flowers in the mouldings run riot. The new national prosperity brought in by Edward IV and later reinforced by Henry VII was having its effect. Money could be and was lavished upon sheer display. The marvel is that so much of this virtuosity is upon a high plane regarded as art. Most of it was expended outside the cathedrals, upon colleges, parish churches and private mansions. But sometimes the cathedrals also benefited, and sometimes by the very finest works of the age. Such was the central or Bell Harry tower added to Canterbury between 1490 and 1497 by John Wastell, Cardinal Morton's master mason. Again striking the exact note required by the whole composition of the cathedral, Wastell's tower is almost as outstanding in its own age as Yevele's nave (147, 161).

The greatest products of the florid Tudor style are Henry VII's Chapel at Westminster Abbey, Wastell's completion of King's College Chapel, and among the cathedrals, Bath. Designed by the brothers Robert and William Vertue for Bishop Oliver King, the church takes up only the site of the nave of the vast Norman abbey. Nothing but the Tudor church is left (150-2). It was an attempt, still within the framework of a Benedictine abbey church, to produce a cathedral upon the lines of a Chapel Royal. As much earlier at Winchester and elsewhere, the fronts are turreted and the aisles depressed. At Bath the aisles are kept to the absolute minimum, while a series of vast clerestory windows achieves the desired glasshouse effect. Final achievement of the English masons, fan-vaults are employed throughout (152). Bath has many beauties, and if it is not one of the most successful of the English cathedrals, the fault lies with its age, rather than in the undoubted genius of the Vertues. But even the common form of the age could have charm, as in Thomas Bertie's remodelling of the Winchester presbytery.

That English architecture was tending to degenerate into lavish frivolities seems to have been widely realized at the time. Especially in the greater domestic architecture there was a strong counter-current of simplicity. Among the cathedrals this movement is found only in one major work, the nave of Ripon, begun in 1503 and finished in less than twenty years. The master was Christopher Scune, who also appears in charge of the building of Louth spire in Lincolnshire, and as master mason at Durham Cathedral. Scune was a man in the tradition of the great masters of construction ; his work is sturdy and well proportioned, and quite devoid of contemporary mannerism (162). The aisles are tall, and their roofs of such low pitch that very little of the clerestory is obscured. Simple and unassuming, the nave would have formed a suitable prelude to the magnificent lancet arches of the new crossing, had that ever been completed. Built in what was then but a poverty-stricken suffragan cathedral, Scune's work cannot rank among the highest flights of Gothic architecture. But it remains one of the most intriguing of our artistic might-have-beens. While the perfected southern architecture was withering before the blasts of the Renaissance, this cruder building of the north was still strong, confident of its own powers. Given a kinder fate, Ripon might have been the germ from which sprang another and still more brilliant English architecture.

The vault of the monastic kitchen at Durham,
with central octagonal opening, 1366–71.

[*Designed by J. Lewyn.*

VI

THE RENAISSANCE AND CONCLUSION

A DOUBLE blow was struck at the English cathedrals by the events of the sixteenth century. The Reformation dissolved the monasteries and jeopardized episcopacy and even the new English cathedral liturgy ; and the Renaissance destroyed the country's living artistic tradition. It might be thought that the alteration in religious outlook would have had the more serious consequences, but this was not so. The Protestant countries of northern Europe, except Holland, all maintained a much greater degree of continuity with their mediaeval tradition than did we. And the reason lies in their modified acceptance of the classical Renaissance. There is no compatibility between the English Gothic of 1525 and the English Mannerism of 1575.

The effects of the religious revolution upon the cathedrals were superficially good rather than bad. Although the monastic bodies were dissolved, no ancient cathedral was destroyed except Coventry ; and five monastic churches (without counting Westminster Abbey) were made cathedral for the first time. All the cathedrals alike now had chapters of secular canons, and these chapters were provided with considerable endowments. But what had been destroyed was one of the chief incentives to building : the belief in the spiritual benefit of pious works which served no obviously practical purpose. One could no longer take out a spiritual insurance policy by endowing a chantry or by making a princely donation to the cathedral fabric fund.

Remarkably little structural work was carried out at any of the cathedrals during the hundred years following the dissolution of the monasteries. The only outstanding exception was Old St. Paul's, where a new portico and a great deal of classic facing were added by Inigo Jones in 1631 to 1640. It is of some interest to note that though in classic style, this new west front adhered to the principles laid down by the Exeter and Winchester porch-screens, of a horizontal mass sweeping across the front and independent of it. Greatly as time-honoured Romanesque and Gothic St. Paul's was reverenced by Londoners, it is clear that it would have been completely classicized in the course of repairs, even had there been no Great Fire.

The state of the structure was already so alarming before the Fire, that a commission of survey, including Wren and Evelyn the diarist, was reporting on the fabric within its last few months of life. Wren had schemes for a central dome in the place of the great tower, and the influence of these pre-Fire plans can be traced in the design finally carried out for the present cathedral. It is profoundly interesting to examine the building to discover the extent to which Wren borrowed from the Gothic tradition in England. In spite of his attempts to force an original and completely un-traditional plan upon the Commissioners, the pressure of tradition was still strong enough to ensure that the new St. Paul's should be an English cathedral, though translated into new architectural terms. The plan, with well-marked transepts, and eastern and western arms both of considerable length, was the first and most fundamental concession to old usage. But no less significant is the section with its flying buttresses, and triforium and clerestory architecturally united. The west front has its towers placed outside the aisles (167), as had been intended at St. Albans and was achieved at Wells and in a half-hearted way at Old St. Paul's itself. East of this typically broad façade were chapels, as at Lincoln and Ely.

It was Ely that provided the inspiration for the central feature of the plan: the eight great piers and the four counter-forts which support the dome (9). Since Wren's uncle was bishop of Ely this is not surprising, but the fact again shows his indebtedness to the basic qualities of Gothic tradition. It is permissible to differ as to the aesthetic values of revived classic buildings in England, but probably few lovers of the English cathedral regard Wren's St. Paul's as altogether in keeping with its spirit. But it is at the same time possible to admire its brilliant composition and construction, and to feel affection for its massed grandeur towering over the spired city that its architect loved.

We would not pull down St. Paul's to rear a sham Gothic structure on its site. And this is because we recognize its greatness in its own kind, and admit its survival value, even should we dislike and disapprove of its detail. Unfortunately, this attitude was not adopted by the church-restorers of last century in their onslaught upon the cathedrals. Not only did they thoroughly " do out " all remains of Renaissance and later alterations and furnishings, but they went so far as to impose a standard of orthodoxy upon Gothic itself. The destruction of a number of fine Perpendicular windows in the interests of a sham Early English purity at St. Albans and elsewhere was the merest vandalism. And the effects of even well-meant surface reconstruction at Chester, Lichfield and Worcester are appalling.

On the other hand, things might be much worse. Even among the rash attacks of the restorers there is a good deal that is informed by a genuine love of Gothic and at least an attempt to grasp its principles. With the possible exception of St. Albans, the victim of Lord Grimthorpe's private massacre, no English cathedral was so severely wrecked as to lose its character. It is

167   St. Paul's : the west front.   Designed by Sir Christopher Wren

169 The south choir aisle, showing part of Tijou's ironwork screen

168 The south nave aisle

unwise to trust to detail for historical purposes without the most careful investigation, but generally speaking the cathedrals do preserve all the main features of their planning and design. In almost every case both the vices and the virtues of the "great" restoration are due to Sir George Gilbert Scott. The exceptions are Bristol and York, where the architect concerned was G. E. Street; Wells, chastened by Anthony Salvin ; Carlisle and South-well, edified by Ewan Christian ; and Southwark, where the new nave is by Sir Arthur Blomfield. Lincoln and Norwich were relatively fortunate in avoiding large-scale works during the nineteenth century.

The losses due to iconoclasm of every kind have been terrible, but so also are those caused merely by lapse of time and by the constant weathering of stone surfaces. Considering that four centuries of wear and tear have gone by since the end of the Gothic period, we must be thankful that so much is left. We should not be human if we did not regret the glories of mediaeval furnishing : the original statues, now so often "restorations" ; the paint-ings ; the immense quantities of woodwork, treasures and plate ; above all, the lost majority of the painted glass. Yet there is still an abundance of skilled craftsmanship left, and a good deal of high art. Dimly as these remains represent what there was in the reign of Henry VIII, the total quantity is still too vast to be set down in detail. The greater works of sculpture can, it is true, be numbered and described ; but the lesser details, the roof-bosses (171-5), the corbel-heads, the little figures and grotesques which pepper the tombs and screens (94, 107, 117, 157, 159), run into many thousands and utterly defy calculation.

Recently Mr. C. J. P. Cave has published a selection of nearly 400 roof-bosses out of a total of over 8,000 telephotographs taken by him. Not all of these were from cathedrals, it is true, but on the other hand there are in the cathedrals many other roof-bosses, and still more carvings of other types. Any one of the major cathedrals would provide work for an average life-time, if every part were to be explored in detail and its stones made to yield up their secrets. Indeed, those who know the cathedrals best, the resident architects, surveyors, clerks of the works and foremen, can from intimate knowledge and affection speak most feelingly of the never-ending multitude of new facts constantly coming to their notice. There is no such thing as "knowing" the whole of a cathedral. But this should not deter anyone from trying to see and to appreciate all that he may.

To give one more example of mere numbers : there are over 700 mediaeval carved misericords in the ancient cathedrals, often some 50 or 60 in one, or even over 100 at Lincoln. On the carved stone screen at Southwell (107) there are over 50 carved heads of appreciable size on one side alone, as well as many more of minute dimensions. The same side of the same screen has over 200 large leaf-crockets, and some 100 foliated capitals or finials. Behind one stall set against this screen is a carved diaper of more than 150 repeats, all different. The quantity of glaziers' work involved can be hinted at by the size of the great west window of Winchester, which alone contains 44 great panels, besides smaller tracery lights. And each of these panels is 8 feet high by nearly 3 feet wide.

Of all the fittings which remain, probably the finest as well as the richest in detail are the series of carved stalls with their canopies and misericord seats. Beginning with some remains of early thirteenth century work at Rochester, and fragments of shafting from canopies at Chichester, we only reach a complete set at Winchester. These were carved by William Lyngwode in 1308-10 ; he had been brought for the purpose from Blofield near Norwich, evidence of his fame. The design with its pierced gables leaps forward from the lancet arcade with level coping which had been used at Westminster Abbey by Jacob the joiner about 1253. The horizontal type of stall canopy was developed at Chichester about 1335, and was united with further elaboration of the gable by William Hurley at Ely in 1336-48. His procedure was to surmount the range of arcading with a second storey of cusped and crocketed tabernacles. At Gloucester between 1337 and 1350 another scheme had been reached by reversal of the Ely design, the tabernacles being above the seats, with a higher range of tracery ending in horizontal cresting. The Ely design was further elaborated about 1370 at Lincoln, almost certainly by William and Hugh Herland, the king's carpenters, Hurley's successors. The rich tabernacle-work then produced was adopted at York and at Chester (164) about 1390, and some time after 1400 at Carlisle. Meanwhile the less popular horizontal design had appeared at Hereford, c. 1380, and increasingly played a part as a motive in tabernacle design at Norwich, c. 1420, and the stalls made by William Brownfleet of Ripon for his own minster, 1489-94 (163), and for the churches of Manchester, c. 1508, and Beverley, 1520. A purely horizontal scheme again appears at Bristol, also made about 1520, and in the Renaissance stalls of Cartmel and King's College, Cambridge ; the triumph of this type under classic influence was complete at new St. Paul's by 1697, and in the stalls of Canterbury Cathedral, made in 1704 and now destroyed. But the final achievement of the Gothic tabernacled design was reserved for Durham, where in 1665 the Restoration bishop, John Cosin, contributed the splendid stalls and fontcover (27) which still exist. These are the only major survivals of post-Reformation fittings in the Gothic cathedrals, but there are many smaller objects of interest of the period 1550-1850 still to be seen, which could only be described in a separate volume.

Naturally the cathedrals differ in richness : some have treasures of all kinds, as Canterbury ; others, like Rochester, have comparatively (but only comparatively) little to offer. In some the architecture is the main attraction ; in others there is a great variety of decorative arts. Canterbury and York are pre-eminent for their glass, and others specially distinguished in this respect are Exeter, Gloucester and Wells ; Winchester, which has a large collection of fragments in its west window ; and Carlisle, where the tracery of the great east window contains some of the richest coloured glass still extant. Canterbury is also famous for wall-paintings, and should be equally noted for its panel-paintings. Winchester, St. Albans and Chichester also contain important wall-paintings, and at Norwich are the remains of a late fourteenth-century painted retable. Lovers of bells will hearken to Great Paul in London, Great Peter in York (a mediaeval bell recast in 1845), and above all to Great Tom of Oxford, brought from Oseney Abbey when the see was moved to Christ Church.

In a category distinct from the decoration, fittings and furniture, stand chantries and monuments (26). Generally speaking they do not form an integral part of the structure, though there are exceptions, such as William of Wykeham's chantry at Winchester, which forms a constructional part of the nave arcade. In other cases, as at Bristol, tomb recesses in the walls form part of the ornamental design of the building (123). The chantries and canopied tombs are frequently of great architectural interest, as they seem often to have served as opportunities for modelling to scale features of fresh design. Experiments in vaulting which could be carried out on a small scale as applied ornament were the basis for much of the later development of the stellar, reticulated and fan vaults (157, 159, 160). And in spite of the destruction wrought at the Reformation and since, the cathedrals (with Westminster Abbey) hold the most important examples of our monuments and tombs of all kinds, from the Norman period to the twentieth century.

This is not the place for a discussion of cathedral services and music, but a few remarks from the historical point of view may not be amiss. The distinctive feature of cathedral services, in common with those of other collegiate churches, is that they are not primarily aimed at the lay worshipper. They are an end subsisting in themselves, and as thoroughly " impractical " as the expenditure of many thousands of pounds upon the building and upkeep of the fabrics. Except where a part of the nave has always been parochial, the custom of having a nave altar with congregational services has no traditional authority, and has no part in the heritage of the cathedral. If this is to be regarded as a falling away from the ancient purity of cathedral worship, there is compensation in the increased and increasing regard for the best music. After centuries of neglect, the great English composers of

Tudor, Elizabethan and Stuart times have been revived, not as mere antiquarianism, but for the splendour of their music on its own merits.

Certain cathedrals have special fame as musical centres, notably the " Three Choirs " of Gloucester, Hereford and Worcester. At the end of the Middle Ages several others were particularly important for their choir-schools, and the famous composers who were organists or choir-masters : Lincoln, London and Wells were all notable in this way, and are again musically notable in the twentieth century. But it would be invidious to single out any cathedrals for praise, where the standard of all is high, and has been so enormously raised within the memory of many now living. From being the land without music, England has rapidly recovered its singing voice, with the cathedrals in the lead. As for instrumental music, there were cathedral orchestras in the Middle Ages, if we accept the evidence of the gallery in the nave at Exeter, and the angels playing upon divers instruments in the Gloucester vault. Great organs have always been found in the English cathedral, since the building of that which in the tenth century at Winchester had four hundred pipes, and required seventy men to blow, and four hands to play.

Music is the art most closely associated with the cathedrals in the public mind ; it is too often forgotten that the cathedral is the embodiment of architecture and its highest expression. That it was also the cause and at the same time the repository of many of the supreme flights of genius in sculpture and painting can be forgotten only too easily, on account of the destruction wrought in the past four centuries. But it is singular that the cathedral should have evoked so little response from English writers. With the exception of a number of passing references in the poetry of the Romantics, mostly of a generalized character, our literature seems to be almost unmarked by the existence of the great churches in our midst. Probably the longest, as well as the finest, passage directly inspired by an English cathedral is the description of St. Hugh's church at Lincoln in the Latin poem on his life written soon after 1220. Amounting to 133 lines, the description not only reaches a high level as literature, but is founded on close observation of detail.

Modern authors have used cathedrals as the setting for dramatic action, but it can hardly be said that the building itself has appealed to their imaginations. Much more attention has, perhaps naturally, been given to the psychology of the cathedral close as a type of society. As often happens, the shortcomings of a way of life have been dwelt upon, and to many who have not lived in a cathedral city the phrase " atmosphere of the Close " conveys an impression of snobbery, servility and petty bickering. Naturally these qualities do exist, as in other societies, but they are not the only qualities. A

170   St. Paul's : the back of Grinling Gibbons' choir stalls

171 Norwich cloister boss, showing the sealing of the Tomb

172 Norwich cloister boss, showing Salome dancing before Herod, and the beheading of St. John the Baptist

173 Wells : boss between the chapter-house doors

174 Chichester : boss in the south choir aisle

175 Norwich cloister boss, showing two stages of the martyrdom of St. Denis under the Emperor Domitian

VAULTING BOSSES

fact commonly overlooked by critics of ecclesiasticism is that high office necessarily calls for administrative capacity. In the nature of things this cannot always, if ever, be linked with other-worldly saintship. But among that hierarchy of bishop, dean, canons, vicars and minor officials that makes up any given Close, there is commonly a saint, an artist, a historian, or a man of letters ; or even all at once. And if not to produce, at least to find a niche for such people, is still as it always has been one of the clearest justifications of the English cathedrals.

Saints are born and not made, but there is a special sense in which the whole of English culture is owed to the cathedrals. The origin of all our education is found in the cathedral school. Some fifty years ago the late A. F. Leach showed that in the Dark and Middle Ages instruction was in the hands, not of the monks, but of the secular clergy. Where the monks maintained schools, it was as the successors of earlier bodies of secular clergy dispossessed in the great monastic movement of late Saxon England. In general, these monastic schools were at the monastic cathedrals ; and at the secular cathedrals the schools pursued their steady course without interruption. The whole of the English school system without exception can be traced back, step by step, to the grammar school of Canterbury Cathedral, first mentioned in A.D. 631. Other cathedral schools which were certainly in existence in the Saxon period were at Rochester, at Winchester, and St. Peter's School at York. There is no reason to doubt that similar schools existed at the remaining cathedrals and greater minsters, and soon after the Norman Conquest there is evidence of many : at Salisbury, Lincoln, Wells, St. Paul's in London, Southwell and Ripon ; and at the monastic cathedrals of Carlisle, Norwich and Worcester. And so it is that whatever there may be of learning and letters in this country, is owed directly or indirectly to the English cathedral.

The work begun by the cathedral schools was carried a stage further by the cathedral libraries. Canterbury, York, Durham and Peterborough were especially famous for their large collections of books, and Hereford still keeps its chained library, reminding us of the extreme value of books when every copy had to be laboriously written by hand. Our first book-collector on a grand scale, Richard of Bury, was a fourteenth-century bishop of Durham. Nowadays perhaps few people would think a cathedral a likely place for a library to be ; still fewer would dream of going to a cathedral library for purposes of study. Yet all our cathedrals are equipped with libraries, some of them still of very great importance for the rare works, both manuscript and printed, in their possession. Outmoded by the modern public libraries for reference and loan, the older institutions have in some cases fallen on evil days, and have but rarely been used even by scholars.

Lately their value has been realized, and they are being assisted by the far-seeing Pilgrim Trust to re-equip themselves. Once again the cathedral library is to take its place as a vital element of English life.

Last, but possibly the greatest of the benefits conferred by the ancient cathedrals, is their function as regional centres : centres of culture, and centres of affection. We have seen how they came into being, each as a focus for the spiritual life of an early kingdom or province. As their number has grown, in accordance with the growth of population, smaller and more precisely defined districts have been provided with such a focus. Every one of them is the spiritual hearth and home of a group of people, the centre of a special devotion and a personal loyalty. According to ties of birth, descent, or domicile, each of us feels one cathedral to be particularly his own. Between all there is a healthy and friendly rivalry. And this particular love is not exclusive : the special affection for one can be heightened by a proper appreciation of all. To each of us belongs our own dear minster ; but the heritage of all of us is the English cathedral.

Chichester : The Bell Tower.

[*Drawn by Roland W. Paul.*

Historical and Descriptive Notes on Each Cathedral

IN these notes the twenty-seven cathedrals are arranged alphabetically. Each note contains a statement of the main facts about the see and foundation ; dimensions of the building; the chief building dates; and, where known, the architects' names. The dimensions are external, except the heights to vault or ceiling ; authorities differ as to dimensions, but the figures given are believed to be approximately correct. Plan dimensions include buttresses ; the width is given across the main transept (eastern transept in the case of Canterbury). Destroyed parts of the buildings are in *italics* ; " (F) " indicates that fragments are visible.

The names of architects given are those of the master craftsmen, where these are known from documentary sources ; names in square brackets indicate strong stylistic evidence. The dates are the *floruit* of each artist, not those of his connection with the individual building. Where no date is given, the evidence is limited to the particular work in question. Dates of building known from documentary evidence are given thus : 1501-39. When the start or finish of work is known, it is shown 1501-, or -1539 ; where the date is known to lie within a given period, it is shown in brackets : (1501-39). Uncertain dates are shown thus: *c.* 1500; *c.* 1501-39, the double date indicating a rather higher degree of probability.

Bath

See : removed from Wells 1090 ; Bath and Glastonbury 1192 ; Bath and Wells 1218.

Foundation : Nunnery 676 ; Secular Canons *c.* 775 ; Benedictine Monks *c.* 970-1539.

Dimensions : length 225 feet ; width 142 feet ; height 75 feet ; tower 162 feet.

Building Dates		Architects
c. 1090-	*Romanesque church* (F)	
c. 1165	*Central tower* completed	
(1248-64)	*Lady Chapel*	
1324-	*Extensive repairs*	Richard Farleigh (1333-63)
c. 1420	*Bubwith's chantry chapel*	
1501-39	Present cathedral	Robert Vertue (1474—d. 1506) ; and William Vertue (1500—d. 1527)
1515-	Prior Bird's chantry	William Vertue ; John Molton (1527—d. 1547)
1864-74	Nave and transept vaults	Sir George Gilbert Scott

BRISTOL

See : 1542 ; united to Gloucester 1836 ; revived 1897.
Foundation : Augustinian Regular Canons 1140-1538 ; a Mitred Abbey 1332-41.
Dimensions : length 338 feet ; width 137 feet ; height 52 feet ; tower 136 feet.

Building Dates		Architects
1140-48	Original church (F) ; gateway to Abbot's lodging	
c. 1154-64	Chapter-house ; great gateway (lower part)	
c. 1220-30	Elder Lady Chapel	
c. 1280	East end and window of Elder Lady Chapel	
c. 1311-40	Choir ; Berkeley and Newton Chapels	
c. 1320	East window	
(1428-73)	Transepts	
c. 1466-71	Central tower	
(1480-1515)	Transept window	
c. 1515-25	Cloisters ; stalls ; south transept vault	
(1481-1526)	Gatehouse over great gateway	
1868-88	Nave and western towers	G. E. Street
1899-1905	Reredos and choir screen	J. L. Pearson

CANTERBURY

See : 597.
Foundation : Secular Canons 597 ; Benedictine Monks 1070-1539.
Dimensions : length 547 feet ; width 171 feet ; height 80 feet ; tower 235 feet.

Building Dates		Architects
1070-77	Lanfranc's church (F)	
c. 1096-1107	Choir ; east transepts (F) ; crypt	Blitherus
1175-78	Choir	William of Sens (1174—d. 1180)
1179-84	Trinity Chapel and corona	William Englishman (1175—d. 1214)
1236-38	Cloister (F)	
1304-20	Screens of choir ; chapter-house (lower part)	[Thomas of Canterbury (1324-35)]
1336	Window of St. Anselm's Chapel	
1341-43	Infirmary table-hall	
c. 1363-	Black Prince's chantry in crypt	? John Box (1350—d. c. 1375)
c. 1372-77	Crypt Lady Chapel	
1379-1405	Nave and south transept	Henry Yevele (1353—d. 1400)
1397-1414	Cloisters	Henry Yevele and Stephen Lote
c. 1400-12	Chapter-house (upper part)	Stephen Lote (1381—d. 1417)
c. 1410	West face of pulpitum	Stephen Lote
1410-39	St. Michael's Chapel	Stephen Lote
c. 1420	South transept vault	
1423-34	South-west tower	Thomas Mapilton (1408—d. 1438)
c. 1440	Henry IV's Chantry	
1448-55	North transept and Lady Chapel	Richard Beke (1409—d. 1458)
1449-68	Tabernacles round south-west tower	
c. 1468	Lady Chapel vault	
1490-97	Central tower and strainer arches in crossing	John Wastell (1493-1515)
c. 1505	Tower vault	John Wastell
1507-17	Christ Church gate	
1834	North-west tower	George Austin

CARLISLE

See : 1133.

Foundation : Secular Canons 1092 ; Augustinian Regular Canons 1123-1540.

Dimensions : length 239 feet ; width 141 feet ; height 72 feet ; tower 110 feet.

Building Dates

(1092-1123)	Nave ; south transept
(1245-92)	Choir, aisles and arcading
1293-1322	Choir, piers and east bay
(1353-95)	Upper walls of choir
(1400-19)	North transept ; tower ; stalls
(1484-1507)	Fratry
1527	Gatehouse

CHESTER

See : 1541

Foundation : Secular Canons before 874-   ; Benedictine Monks 1093-1540.

Dimensions : length 371 feet ; width 206 feet ; height 75 feet ; tower 127 feet.

Building Dates   *Architects*

1093-1140	North transept ; north-west tower	
1194-c. 1250	Presbytery ; chapter-house ; refectory	
(1265-90)	Lady Chapel	
c. 1283-1315	Choir	Richard Lenginour (1277-1320)
c. 1323-	Nave (part) ; south transept (part)	
c. 1390	Stalls	
(1485-92)	Nave, north arcade	
(1493-1537)	Central tower ; south transept ; porch	
1508-37	South-west tower	
(c. 1500-30)	Cloisters	

CHICHESTER

See : (at Selsey 709) ; removed to Chichester 1075.

Foundation : Secular Canons.

Dimensions : length 408 feet ; width 157 feet ; height 61 feet ; spire 277 feet

Building Dates   *Architects*

1088-1108	Presbytery	
1114-23	East nave	
(1123-48)	West nave ; south-west tower	
1187-99	Retrochoir ; recasing and vaulting	Walter of Coventry
(1215-25)	South-west tower (upper stage)	
(c. 1225-50)	South chapels and north-east chapels of nave	
c. 1244-47	Central tower	
(c. 1250-75)	North-west chapels of nave ; west porch	
(1288-1304)	Lady Chapel, eastern bays	
(1305-37)	South transept remodelled	
(1391-1402)	Spire completed	John Mason
1396	Vicars' Hall	
c. 1410-40	Campanile	
(c. 1400-1500)	Cloisters	
1861-66	Central tower and spire rebuilt	Sir G. G. Scott
1899-1901	North-west tower	J. L. Pearson

DURHAM

See : (Lindisfarne 635 ; Chester-le-Street 883) ; removed to Durham 997.
Foundation : Celtic Monks 995 ; Secular Canons ? ; Benedictine Monks 1093–1540.
Dimensions : length 502 feet ; width 192 feet ; height 74 feet ; tower 218 feet.

Building Dates		Architects
1093–99	Choir	
1099–1128	Nave	
1128–33	Nave vault	
1133–40	Chapter-house	
c. 1170	Galilee	Richard Wolveston (1170—d. c. 1182)
c. 1220	West towers (upper stages)	
1242–80	Chapel of Nine Altars	Richard Farnham (1242–47)
c. 1341	West window	? Roger Mason
1366–71	Kitchen	John Lewyn (1364—d. c. 1398)
1375–80	Reredos (Neville screen)	? Henry Yevele (1353—d. 1400) and John Lewyn
1390–1418	Cloisters	John Lewyn ; Thomas Mapilton (1408—d. 1438)
1465–75	Central tower (lower stage)	? Thomas Barton
c. 1483–90	Central tower (upper stage)	John Bell, junior (1478–88)

ELY

See : 1109.
Foundation : Benedictine Nuns 673 ; Benedictine Monks 970–1540.
Dimensions : length 537 feet ; width 199 feet ; height 86 feet ; western tower 215 feet.

Building Dates		Architects
1083–1106	*Choir and central tower*	
c. 1090–1130	Transepts and nave	
c. 1174–97	West transept and tower	
(1198–1215)	Galilee porch	
1239–50	Retrochoir	
1325	Prior Crauden's Chapel	
1321–49	Lady Chapel	
1322–36	Choir	
1322–46	Octagon	John (? Ramsey) and John Atte Grene (1334–57)
1328–40	Vault and lantern	William Hurley (1326—d. 1354)
1336–48	Stalls	William Hurley
1371–74	Lady Chapel, east window	Thomas Ufford
1387–90	*Reredos*	Robert Wodehirst (1351—d. 1401)
1392–	? Lantern of west tower	Robert Wodehirst
1396–1400	Great gatehouse (porta)	John Meppushal (1374–1418)
1474–78	Arches beneath west tower	Thomas Peyntour (1471–95)
(1486–1500)	Bishop Alcock's Chapel	? Adam Lord (*fl.* 1490)
1509–10	Cloisters, east walk	Thomas Palmer (1505–)
1534	Bishop West's Chapel	

EXETER

See : (Crediton 909) ; removed to Exeter 1049.
Foundation : Benedictine Monks ?–1003 and 1019–49 ; Secular Canons 1049– .
Dimensions : length 409 feet ; width 158 feet ; height 69 feet ; towers 130 feet.

Building Dates		*Architects*
(1112-36)	Towers	
(1224-44)	Chapter-house	? Alexander FitzJohn
c. 1275-	Lady Chapel and retrochoir	
1288-1308	Presbytery ; Lady Chapel vaults	Roger (1299-1310)
1308-17	Crossing ; nave, east bay	William Luve (1310-16)
1309-17	Stalls ; bishop's throne	John of Glaston and Thomas of Winton
1316-24	High altar ; reredos and sedilia ; pulpitum	Thomas Witney (1316-42)
1323-24	*Cloister, east walk*	Thomas Witney
1328-42	Nave	Thomas Witney
1330-32	*Cloister, north walk*	Thomas Witney
1346-75	Screen of west front	William Joy (1329-46)
(1353-69)	Nave vault	Richard Farleigh (1333-63)
1376-82	*Cloister, south and west walks*	Robert Lesyngham (1376-94)
1390-91	East window	Robert Lesyngham
1413-39	Chapter-house (upper part)	John Tynlegh (*fl.* 1412) ; John Harry (1407—d. *c.* 1455)
(1504-19)	Oldham and Speke chantry chapels	

GLOUCESTER

See : 1541 ; united with Bristol 1836 ; separated 1897.
Foundation : Benedictine Monks and Nuns 681 ; Secular Priests 823 ; Benedictine Monks 1022-1539.
Dimensions : length 425 feet ; width 154 feet ; height 86 feet ; tower 225 feet.

Building Dates		*Architects*
1089-1100	Crypt and choir	
c. 1100-60	Nave	
1242-45	Nave vault	? John of Gloucester (1245—d. 1260)
(1318-29)	Nave, south aisle	
(1331-37)	South transept remodelled	
(1337-50)	Choir remodelled ; stalls	[William Ramsey (1326—d. 1349)]
1368-74	North transept remodelled	[Robert Lesyngham (1376-94)]
c. 1370-77	Cloister, six south bays east walk	[Robert Lesyngham]
(1381-1412)	Cloisters completed	
(1421-37)	West front and two bays ; south porch	
1450-60	Central tower	? John Hobbs (1455-75)
(1457-83)	Lady Chapel	? John Hobbs

HEREFORD

See : 676.
Foundation : Secular Canons.
Dimensions : length 344 feet ; width 177 feet ; height 64 feet ; tower 165 feet.

Building Dates		*Architects*
1079-1110	Choir ; south transept (part)	
c. 1100-45	Nave and transepts	
c. 1190	Vestibule of Lady Chapel	
c. 1220	Lady Chapel	
c. 1250-68	North transept ; choir clerestory and vault ; inner north porch	
(1283-1316)	Aisle walls	Hugh Mason (*fl.* 1291)
c. 1325	Central tower	
1364-70	*Chapter-house* (F)	Thomas Cambridge
c. 1400	South transept vault	

6

Building Dates		Architects
1412-18	Cloister (part)	Thomas Denyar
c. 1470	Bishop Stanbury's chantry chapel	
c. 1500	Bishop Audley's chantry ; vicars' cloister	
c. 1520-30	Outer north porch	
1908	West front	J. Oldrid Scott

LICHFIELD

See : 669 (Archbishopric 787-803) ; removed to Chester 1075 ; to Coventry 1095 ; Coventry and Lichfield 1148 ; Lichfield and Coventry 1539 ; Lichfield 1836.
Foundation : Secular Canons.
Dimensions : length 397 feet ; width 177 feet ; height 57 feet ; central spire 258 feet.

Building Dates		Architects
1195-1208	Choir arcades	
c. 1220-40	Transepts	
(1239-49)	Chapter-house and vestibule	Thomas (c. 1230-50)
c. 1250-80	Nave	? William FitzThomas (c. 1250-65)
c. 1280-93	West front (lower part)	? Thomas Wallace (c. 1265-80)
(1294-1327)	West front (upper part)	
c. 1300	Central tower	
c. 1320-36	Lady Chapel	William of Eyton (1322-36)
1337-	Presbytery	William Ramsey (1326—d. 1349)
1385-	? Spires	Gilbert Mason
1661-69	General restoration	Sir William Wilson

LINCOLN

See : (Lindsey 678 ; removed to Dorchester, Oxon. 958) ; Lincoln 1073.
Foundation : Secular Canons.
Dimensions : length 512 feet ; width 251 feet ; height 82 feet ; tower 271 feet.

Building Dates		Architects
1074-92	Centre of west front	
c. 1140-50	West doorways ; west towers (lower parts)	
1192-1200	Choir and east transept	(Geoffrey de Noyers) ; Richard Mason (fl. c. 1190)
c. 1200-20	Great transept	? Michael (fl. c. 1210-30)
c. 1220-35	Chapter-house	Alexander (1235-48)
c. 1225-53	Nave ; west front ; Galilee	Alexander
1238-	Central tower (lower part)	Alexander
1256-80	Angel choir	Simon of Thirsk (c. 1275-90)
c. 1296-	Cloisters	? Richard of Stow
1306-11	Central tower (upper part)	Richard of Stow (1291-1311)
c. 1320	South transept gable with " Bishop's Eye "	
c. 1370	Stalls ; statues over west door, etc.	
c. 1370-1400	West towers (upper parts)	? Geoffrey (fl. 1359)
c. 1431	Bishop Fleming's chantry chapel	
c. 1493	Bishop Russell's chantry chapel	
c. 1548	Bishop Longland's chantry chapel	? William Kitchin (1528-59)

LONDON

See : 604.
Foundation : Secular Canons.

Old St. Paul's.

Dimensions : length 644 feet ; width 315 feet ; height 103 feet ; spire 520 feet.

Building Dates		Architects
c. 1090–	Choir	
c. 1110–30	Nave begun	Andrew Mason (fl. 1127)
(1137–1200)	Restorations after fire	
c. 1200–21	Tower	
1251–c. 1300	New work of choir	
1256–	Transepts	
1332–	Chapter-house and cloister (F)	William Ramsey (1326—d. 1349)
1374–76	Tomb of John of Gaunt	Henry Yevele (1353—d. 1400)
1382–87	South transept front	Henry Yevele
1388–	? Pulpitum	Henry Yevele
1631–40	West portico ; refacing	Inigo Jones
(1686)	Demolition completed	

New St. Paul's.

Dimensions : length 510 feet ; width 140 feet ; height 89 feet ; dome to top of cross 366 feet.

Building Dates		Architect
1675–1710	(Complete to top of lantern)	Sir Christopher Wren

NORWICH

See : (Dunwich 631 ; Elmham 673 ; Thetford 1070) ; removed to Norwich 1094.
Foundation : Benedictine Monks 1095–1539.
Dimensions : length 481 feet (inclusive of thirteenth-century Lady Chapel) ; width 190 feet ; height 83 feet ; spire 320 feet.

Building Dates		Architects
1096–1120	Choir and transepts	
c. 1121–45	Nave and tower	
c. 1175–1200	Completion after fire	
c. 1272–78	St. Ethelbert gate	? Bartholomew Massingham (1265)
1272–90	Lady Chapel	? Bartholomew Massingham
1289–1303	Chapter-house	Richard (? Curteys/Ramsey) (1285–90)
1297–1325	Cloister, east walk ; windows of north nave aisle	John Ramsey (1304–39)
1327–50	Cloister, south walk	William Ramsey (1326—d. 1349)
c. 1362–69	Presbytery clerestory	? Robert Wodehirst (1351—d. 1401)
1385–89	Cloister, continued	? Robert Wodehirst
1416–25	Erpingham gate	James Wodrove (1415–51)
1416–26	Cloister, west walk	James Wodrove
1421–30	Cloister, north walk	James Wodrove
1426–36	West front ; inserted windows	? James Wodrove
c. 1463–72	Nave vault	? John Everard (1437–75)
c. 1472–99	Presbytery vault ; flying buttresses	? John Everard
c. 1501–36	Catton screen ; Nykke's chantry ; transept vaults	

6*

OXFORD

See : (in Oseney Abbey 1542) ; removed to Christ Church 1546.
Foundation : Nuns 727-1049 ; Secular Canons 1049-1111 ; Augustinian Regular
Canons 1111-1524.
Dimensions : length 187 feet ; width 111 feet ; height 44 feet ; spire 144 feet.

Building Dates		*Architects*
1158-80	Church ; tower (lower stage)	
c. 1220-50	Tower (upper stage and spire) ; chapter-house ; Lady Chapel	
c. 1350-55	Latin Chapel	
(1478-1503)	Choir vault ; cloisters	? William Orchard (1475—d. 1504)
1525-29	Hall and Tom Quad	John Lebons (1506-37) and Henry Redman (1509—d. 1528)

PETERBOROUGH

See : 1541.
Foundation : Benedictine Monks 654-870 ; 972-1539.
Dimensions : length 481 feet ; width 206 feet ; height 81 feet ; tower 143 feet.

Building Dates		*Architects*
1117—c. 1155	Choir and transept	
c. 1155-75	Nave	
c. 1177-93	West transept	
c. 1193-1220	West front	
1272-86	*Lady Chapel* (F)	
c. 1325	Central tower	
c. 1375	Galilee porch	
c. 1475	*Cloisters* (F)	? John Kilham (1473-88)
c. 1496-1508	New building	[John Wastell (1493-1515)]

RIPON

See : 1836.
Foundation : Celtic Monks 657-664 ; Benedictine Monks 664-948 ; Secular Canons
before 1066- .
Dimensions : length 297 feet ; width 156 feet ; height 94 feet ; towers 121 feet.

Building Dates		*Architects*
(1154-81)	Transepts ; *nave* (F)	? Arthur Mason (*fl. c.* 1190)
c. 1230-40	West front and towers	
(1288-97)	East end of choir	
c. 1482	Choir, two west bays of south side ; pulpitum	
1489-94	Stalls	William Brownfleet (1489-1523)
1502-22	Nave	Christopher Scune (1505-21)

ROCHESTER

See : 604.
Foundation : Secular Canons 604-1076 ; Benedictine Monks 1076-1540.
Dimensions : length 324 feet ; width 146 feet ; height 55 feet ; spire 156 feet.

Building Dates

(1077-1108)	Church (F) ; north tower
c. 1115-30	Nave
c. 1150	West front
c. 1200-27	Presbytery ; east transept ; choir
c. 1240-55	North transept
c. 1280-	South transept ; nave, two east bays
(1319-52)	Chapter-house doorway ; central tower
c. 1470	West window
c. 1490	Nave clerestory
c. 1512	Lady Chapel

ST. ALBANS

See : 1878.

Foundation : Benedictine Monks 793-1539.

Dimensions : length 550 feet ; width 191 feet ; height 70 feet ; tower 144 feet.

Building Dates		*Architects*
1077-1115	Norman church and tower	Robert Mason
(1195-1214)	West front (part)	Hugh Goldcliff
(1214-35)	West front completed ; west bays of nave	
1257-c. 1290	Presbytery	
(1260-1326)	Ante-chapel	
c. 1302-08	Shrine of St. Alban	
(1308-26)	Lady Chapel	
1314-	Stalls	Geoffrey
1324-27	Nave, five bays of south side	Henry Wy
c. 1360-90	Great gatehouse ; nave screen	? Henry Yevele (1353—d. 1400)
(1447)	Tomb of Humphrey Duke of Gloucester	? John Wolvey (1428—d. 1462)
(1476-84)	Reredos	
(1492-1521)	Abbot Ramryge's chantry	

SALISBURY

See : (Sherborne 705 ; Ramsbury [920] and Sherborne 1058) ; removed to Old Sarum c. 1075 ; Salisbury 1228.

Foundation : Secular Canons.

Dimensions : length 473 feet ; width 230 feet ; height 84 feet ; spire 404 feet.

Building Dates		*Architects*
1220-25	Lady Chapel	(Elias of Dereham) ; Nicholas of Ely
1225-37	Choir	(Elias of Dereham) ; Nicholas of Ely
1237-58	Great transept ; nave	(Elias of Dereham) ; Nicholas of Ely
c. 1258-66	West front	Richard Mason (1267)
c. 1263-84	Chapter-house and cloister	Richard Mason
1334-c. 1380	Tower and spire	Richard Farleigh (1333-63)
(1387-1400)	? Strainer arches in east transepts	Nicholas Portland
(1417-23)	? Strainer arches beneath tower	Robert Wayte

SOUTHWARK

See : 1905.

Foundation : Nuns ? ; Secular Canons 852 ; Augustinian Regular Canons 1106-1540.

Dimensions : length 262 feet ; width 130 feet ; height 55 feet ; tower 163 feet.

Building Dates		*Architects*
c. 1208–35	Choir and retrochoir	
c. 1273–	Transepts ; nave	
c. 1385–1405	*West front* ; tower	? Henry Yevele (1353—d. 1400
c. 1420	South transept altered	
c. 1520	Reredos	
1889–97	Nave	Sir Arthur Blomfield

SOUTHWELL

See : 1884.
Foundation : Secular Canons.
Dimensions : length 318 feet ; width 137 feet ; height 50 feet ; tower 105 feet.

Building Dates	
(1108–50)	Transepts and nave
c. 1230–50	Eastern arm
c. 1293–1300	Chapter-house
c. 1330	Pulpitum
c. 1450	West window

WELLS

See : 909 ; removed to Bath 1090 ; Bath and Wells 1218.
Foundation : Secular Canons.
Dimensions : length 415 feet ; width 153 feet ; height 67 feet ; tower 182 feet.

Building Dates		*Architects*
(1174–92)	Choir	
(1192–c. 1206)	Transept ; nave ; north porch	
c. 1220–39	West front	Adam Lock (d. 1229)
c. 1275–86	Undercroft of chapter-house	
c. 1293–1319	Chapter-house ; Lady Chapel	
c. 1321	Central tower	
c. 1329–	Retrochoir ; choir reconstructed	William Joy (1329–46)
c. 1338	" St. Andrew's Arches " under tower	William Joy
1365–90	South-west tower	William Wynford (1360–1403)
c. 1410–35	North-west tower	
c. 1443–58	Cloisters	? John Turpyn
c. 1470–91	*Cloister Lady Chapel* (F)	William Smyth (d. 1490) ; William Atwood (1490–98)

WINCHESTER

See : (Dorchester, Oxon. 635) ; removed to Winchester c. 679.
Foundation : Secular Canons c. 679 ; Benedictine Monks 963–1540.
Dimensions : length 554 feet ; width 231 feet ; height 78 feet ; tower 140 feet.

Building Dates		*Architects*
1079–93	Crypt ; transepts	
1108–20	Tower and north and south bays adjoining	
1202–c. 1235	Retrochoir and Lady Chapel	
1308–10	Stalls	William Lyngwode
c. 1320–60	Presbytery	
c. 1360	West front with two bays of north aisle and one bay of south aisle	

Building Dates		Architects
1394-c. 1450	Nave ; Wykeham's Chapel	William Wynford (1360-1403) ; Robert Hulle (1412-c. 1440)
c. 1475-80	Reredos	
c. 1490-1500	Lady Chapel ; eastern bay and vault	
c. 1520-32	Presbytery : aisles, screens and clere-story ; Fox's chantry	Thomas Bertie (1501—d. 1555)

WORCESTER

See : 680.

Foundation : Secular Canons 680 ; Benedictine Monks c. 970-1539.

Dimensions : length 425 feet ; width 147 feet ; height 68 feet ; tower 196 feet.

Building Dates		Architects
1084-92	Crypt	
c. 1120	Chapter-house	
c. 1170	Nave, two western bays	
1224-	Choir and retrochoir	Alexander Mason
1317-24	Nave, five East bays on north	William of Shockerwick (fl. 1316)
c. 1360-74	Nave, two bays on north and seven on south ; cloister ; tower	John Clyve (1362-76)
1375-95	Vaults of nave and crossing ; west front ; north porch	John Clyve
c. 1400	Chapter-house : door, windows, buttresses	
1502-04	Prince Arthur's chantry chapel	

YORK

See : 625.

Foundation : Secular Canons.

Dimensions : length 524 feet ; width 244 feet ; height 102 feet ; tower 213 feet.

Building Dates		Architects
(1154-81)	Crypt	
(1220-41)	South transept	
(1245-60)	North transept	
(1286-1307)	Chapter-house	
1291-1345	Nave ; west front	Simon Mason (1301—d. 1322)
c. 1330-38	West window	? Thomas Pakenham
1354-70	Nave vault (wood)	Philip Lincoln (1346-75)
1361-73	Lady Chapel : four bays	Robert Patrington (1353-71)
(1380-1400)	Choir : five west bays	Hugh Hedon (1399-1408)
c. 1400-05	East window	Hugh Hedon
1407-23	Central tower	William Colchester (1400—d. 1420)
1432-56	South-west tower	Thomas Pak (1420-41)
1470-74	North-west tower	William Hyndeley (1466—d. 1505)
1475-1500	Rood screen	William Hyndeley

THE DESCENT OF ARCHITECTURAL FEATURES

The following tables and charts are intended to show at a glance the historical growth or various types of certain architectural features. In every case the date given approximates to that of design, not necessarily that of construction.

RIBBED VAULTS

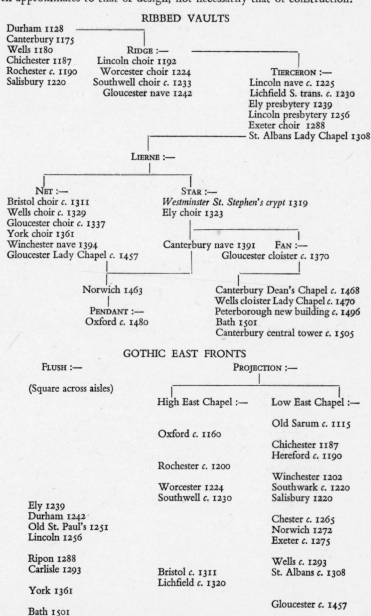

Durham 1128
Canterbury 1175
Wells 1180
Chichester 1187
Rochester *c.* 1190
Salisbury 1220

RIDGE :—
Lincoln choir 1192
Worcester choir 1224
Southwell choir *c.* 1233
Gloucester nave 1242

TIERCERON :—
Lincoln nave *c.* 1225
Lichfield S. trans. *c.* 1230
Ely presbytery 1239
Lincoln presbytery 1256
Exeter choir 1288
St. Albans Lady Chapel 1308

LIERNE :—

NET :—
Bristol choir *c.* 1311
Wells choir *c.* 1329
Gloucester choir *c.* 1337
York choir 1361
Winchester nave 1394
Gloucester Lady Chapel *c.* 1457

STAR :—
Westminster St. Stephen's crypt 1319
Ely choir 1323

Canterbury nave 1391   FAN :—
Gloucester cloister *c.* 1370

Norwich 1463

PENDANT :—
Oxford *c.* 1480

Canterbury Dean's Chapel *c.* 1468
Wells cloister Lady Chapel *c.* 1470
Peterborough new building *c.* 1496
Bath 1501
Canterbury central tower *c.* 1505

GOTHIC EAST FRONTS

FLUSH :—

(Square across aisles)

PROJECTION :—

High East Chapel :—

Low East Chapel :—

Oxford *c.* 1160

Old Sarum *c.* 1115

Chichester 1187
Hereford *c.* 1190

Rochester *c.* 1200

Winchester 1202
Southwark *c.* 1220
Salisbury 1220

Worcester 1224
Southwell *c.* 1230

Ely 1239
Durham 1242
Old St. Paul's 1251
Lincoln 1256

Chester *c.* 1265
Norwich 1272
Exeter *c.* 1275

Ripon 1288
Carlisle 1293

Wells *c.* 1293
St. Albans *c.* 1308

York 1361

Bristol *c.* 1311
Lichfield *c.* 1320

Bath 1501

Gloucester *c.* 1457

Note.—Canterbury is in a class by itself, in no way resembling any other cathedral in its eastern termination. Peterborough has a square series of *low* eastern chapels.

WEST FRONTS

No towers	Towers on aisle axes	Towers outside aisles
	Lincoln *c.* 1074	
	Chester *c.* 1100	
Hereford *c.* 1100 [1]	Durham *c.* 1100	
	Chichester *c.* 1125	
	Southwell *c.* 1130	
Rochester *c.* 1150		Old St. Paul's *c.* 1150
Worcester *c.* 1170		(Ely *c.* 1174) [2]
		Peterborough *c.* 1177
		St. Albans *c.* 1195
		Wells *c.* 1220
		(Ripon *c.* 1230) [3]
Salisbury *c.* 1258		(Lincoln W. transept
	Lichfield *c.* 1280	*c.* 1230)
	York 1291	
Exeter 1328		
Winchester *c.* 1360		
	Canterbury 1379	
Gloucester *c.* 1421		
Norwich 1426		
Bath 1501		

The place of the type with outside towers was taken by the horizontal porch-range or screen-front, as below.

SCREEN FRONTS AND WELCOMING PORCHES

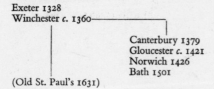

Exeter 1328
Winchester *c.* 1360

Canterbury 1379
Gloucester *c.* 1421
Norwich 1426
Bath 1501

(Old St. Paul's 1631)

[1] Hereford had a single western tower, not at first planned.
[2] Ely has a single tower, with a projecting western transept.
[3] Ripon had no aisles, but a broad nave with three western doors between the towers.

GREAT TOWERS

The number of windows in the main stage is shown in brackets.

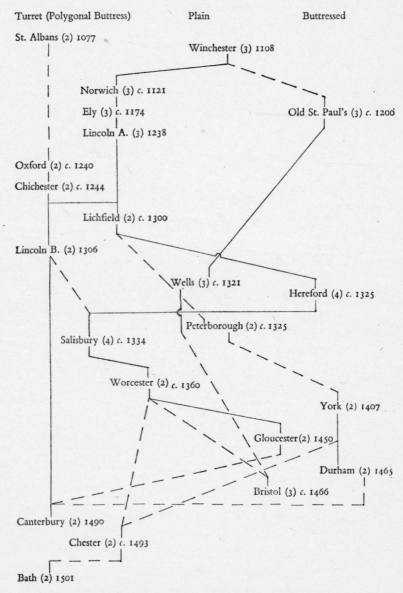

Turret (Polygonal Buttress)   Plain   Buttressed

St. Albans (2) 1077

Winchester (3) 1108

Norwich (3) c. 1121

Ely (3) c. 1174   Old St. Paul's (3) c. 1200

Lincoln A. (3) 1238

Oxford (2) c. 1240

Chichester (2) c. 1244

Lichfield (2) c. 1300

Lincoln B. (2) 1306

Wells (3) c. 1321

Hereford (4) c. 1325

Peterborough (2) c. 1325

Salisbury (4) c. 1334

Worcester (2) c. 1360

York (2) 1407

Gloucester (2) 1450

Durham (2) 1465

Bristol (3) c. 1466

Canterbury (2) 1490

Chester (2) c. 1493

Bath (2) 1501

Note.—Influences from outside the cathedral group of towers were strong in some cases, notably at Bath. The later towers are eclectic and not precisely classifiable.

POLYGONAL CHAPTER-HOUSES

The number of sides (or bays) is shown in brackets.

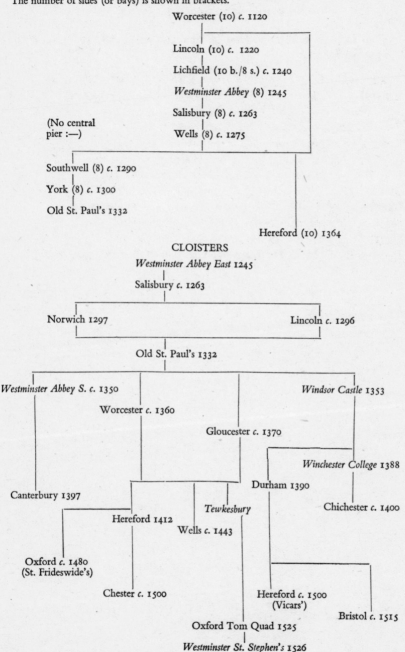

Worcester (10) *c.* 1120

Lincoln (10) *c.* 1220

Lichfield (10 b./8 s.) *c.* 1240

Westminster Abbey (8) 1245

Salisbury (8) *c.* 1263

(No central
pier :—)

Wells (8) *c.* 1275

Southwell (8) *c.* 1290

York (8) *c.* 1300

Old St. Paul's 1332

Hereford (10) 1364

CLOISTERS

Westminster Abbey East 1245

Salisbury *c.* 1263

Norwich 1297

Lincoln *c.* 1296

Old St. Paul's 1332

Westminster Abbey S. c. 1350

Worcester *c.* 1360

Gloucester *c.* 1370

Windsor Castle 1353

Winchester College 1388

Durham 1390

Canterbury 1397

Tewkesbury

Chichester *c.* 1400

Hereford 1412

Wells *c.* 1443

Oxford *c.* 1480
(St. Frideswide's)

Chester *c.* 1500

Hereford *c.* 1500
(Vicars')

Bristol *c.* 1515

Oxford Tom Quad 1525

Westminster St. Stephen's 1526

BIBLIOGRAPHICAL NOTE

This includes only a selection of the most useful modern books dealing with the subject.

ATKINSON, T. D. : *English and Welsh Cathedrals,* 1912.

BATSFORD, H. and FRY, C. : *The Cathedrals of England,* 1936, etc.

—— *The Greater English Church,* 1940, etc.

BELL, E., ed. : *Bell's Cathedral Series.*

BOND, F. : *Gothic Architecture in England,* 1906.

—— *The Cathedrals of England and Wales,* 1912.

—— *An Introduction to English Church Architecture,* 1913.

BUILDER, THE : *Cathedrals of England and Wales,* 1894.

BUMPUS, T. F. : *The Cathedrals of England and Wales,* 1926.

Notes on the Cathedrals Series (S.P.C.K.).

PRIOR, E. S. : *The Cathedral Builders in England,* 1905.

THOMPSON, A. H. : *The Cathedral Churches of England,* 1925.

INDEX

THE captions of the plates have been included, and also the names of architects occurring in the Notes. Numerals in **heavy type** refer to the *figure numbers* of the illustrations; *italic* numerals refer to the *pages* on which line-blocks occur.